Like a Shadow
That
Never Departs

THE STORY OF ANANDA:
THE BUDDHA'S CHIEF-OF-STAFF

Randall K. Scott

LIKE A SHADOW THAT NEVER DEPARTS
THE STORY OF ANANDA: THE BUDDHA'S CHIEF-OF-STAFF

iUniverse books may be ordered through booksellers or by contacting:

iUniverse
1663 Liberty Drive
Bloomington, IN 47403
www.iuniverse.com
844-349-9409

Because of the dynamic nature of the Internet, any web addresses or links contained in this book may have changed since publication and may no longer be valid. The views expressed in this work are solely those of the author and do not necessarily reflect the views of the publisher, and the publisher hereby disclaims any responsibility for them.

Any people depicted in stock imagery provided by Getty Images are models, and such images are being used for illustrative purposes only.
Certain stock imagery © Getty Images.

ISBN: 978-1-6632-3043-0 (sc)
ISBN: 978-1-6632-3044-7 (e)

Library of Congress Control Number: 2021921478

Print information available on the last page.

iUniverse rev. date: 11/29/2021

Dedication

To Marc'a, who introduced me to Buddhism,
and shows me how it should be practiced by her actions every day.

Professor Randall Scott's book *'Like a shadow that does not depart"* is a highly informative and very interesting story of Ananda, Buddha's Chief-of-Staff for 25 years. The title is Ananda's beautiful description of his intimate and constant positive relationship with Buddha. Scott provides psychological insight and historical perspective on Buddha and Ananda and their relationship. Ananda influenced Buddha to admit women to monastic life which was a historic step, and it was Ananda's unique capacity to memorize and recall Buddha's speeches that preserved them intact. Scott explains various Buddhist terms. This book deserves wide readership among people interested in religion and spirituality in general and Buddhism in particular.

N.S. Xavier, M.D., author of *The Two Faces of Religion* and *Fulfillment Using Real Conscience.*

Contents

Acknowledgments

Thanks to N.S. Xavier, M.D. for his valuable
insights and gracious advice.
Thanks to my wife, Marc'a for her unflagging support.

Introduction

Ananda is described in writings of the time as the Buddha's attendant. But he was much more than a mere servant. He was the Buddha's confidant and friend. I explore why and how the close personal relationship between the two men resulted in Ananda gaining and exercising enormous power over the sangha.

The humanity of the Buddha and his followers attracted me to this project. The Buddha never claimed to be a god. He and his disciples struggled with the same desires, attachments, jealousies, and illnesses as his followers. Consequently, a very keen understanding of the human condition runs through Buddhist writings. Modern readers will recognize the obstacles disciples had to overcome daily in their journey to nirvana; because we face the same problems today---two thousand five hundred years since the Buddha lived and spoke.

Reconstructing historical events can be challenging; especially if the events and conversations are recalled totally from memory when there were no written records. Eyewitness recollections are notoriously unreliable. "Historical sources often supply us with varying accounts. This probably stems from irregularities in what people saw or heard, resulting in different recorded accounts and as the story spreads the accounts naturally increase. It is like different people looking at the sun or moon from different positions; the sun and moon are the same, but the differences in the clouds and surroundings make them appear different"[1]

Akira Kurosawa's classic *Rashomon* (1950) showed how several participants and witnesses to a murder had conflicting memories of the incident. When I was an undergraduate many years ago, I was in a criminal justice class when three young men burst into the classroom and dragged a student out, kicking and screaming. Of course, it was all staged so the instructor could show us the problems with eyewitness testimony; and it was effective. Everyone seemed to have a different view of the incident. Thus, conflicting accounts of historical events must be resolved. When scholars disagreed about Ananda's age or the content of specific conversations or the size of a crowd or other eyewitness reports, I tried to triangulate the available information to arrive at the most plausible answer.

I adhere to the traditional scholarly/academic practice of listing sources, but to improve readability and flow, I have not footnoted commonly accepted historical facts about Buddhism. However, if I quote a particularly relevant conversation between the Buddha and Ananda or a pertinent observation by another researcher, I clearly footnote. My sources are easily available to English-language readers. The spelling of Buddhist phrases might differ according to whether the sources are translated from Sanskrit or Pali.

My purpose is to explore the life of Ananda; but attention must be given to the Buddha, his disciples, and specific Buddhist principles to provide context and a back-story for Ananda. As a result, descriptions of the Four Noble Truths, the Noble Eightfold Path, Nirvana, dependent arising, samsara, emptiness, and other important Buddhist principles are, by necessity condensed but not superficial. Terms that might increase the reader's knowledge and enjoyment are defined in the glossary. There are myriad sources to explore Buddhism in greater depth. A lot has been written about Buddhism in the last two thousand five hundred years.

The Buddha was not just an ordinary man with extraordinary talents. He was far from that. He was a unique man, who, at the age of twenty-nine, left his wife and newborn son and a life of luxury to become a wandering mendicant. After six years of experimentation with extreme fasting that nearly killed him, he found a way to transcend this world filled with suffering forever. Siddhartha Gautama became enlightened and became the Buddha. But that wasn't the end of his journey. He had to choose whether to enter nirvana immediately or to teach others what he had discovered. He chose to pay it forward by walking for the remaining forty-five years of his life through what is now northern India and Tibet teaching the Four Noble Truths and the Noble Eightfold Path. From the time of his enlightenment until his parinirvanization, it is estimated that the Buddha "rescued ...a hundred-thousand beings from the ocean of samsara and established them on the shore, that is, nibbana.[2]

Why did the Buddha and his disciples choose to walk on their pilgrimages when chariots and carts were available? The Buddha wanted to show that he was physically here; so, he left a spiritual path, his footprints, that we can follow to enlightenment. There are thousands of casts of the Buddha's footprints throughout India and Asia. Of course, it is unlikely that all are the Buddha's, but the symbolism is powerful.

The Buddha needed disciples to help him spread the religion. The character of a leader can be judged by the company he keeps. A strong, moral, ethical leader surrounds himself with strong, moral, ethical subordinates. The Buddha's inner circle was almost exclusively enlightened arhats with one notable exception---Ananda. But as this book reveals, Ananda was often the moral and ethical compass for the sangha when the arhats displayed troubling fits of clearly unenlightened behaviors such as gossiping, back-biting, and jealousy. Women had no rights, as we think of them, during this period. But Ananda strongly supported an order of nuns.[3] Ananda was the conscience of the sangha.

Ananda played a pivotal role in Buddhism's growth. In an age when nothing was written down; remarkable, gifted men like Ananda devoted their lives to hearing and memorizing the Buddha's discourses exactly as the Buddha voiced them so his teachings would not be lost.

I did not expect the Buddha or his sangha to behave like twenty-first century men. I report their actions from the viewpoint and social customs of people who lived two-and-a-half millennia ago during an extremely patriarchal period. Nevertheless, I found Ananda's and the Buddha's attitude toward women's rights surprisingly modern. The Buddha has been accused of being a misogynist or anti-female; but an objective analysis of the evidence indicates that the Buddha did not hate women. He just felt that women would interfere in the celibate monks' mindfulness and would delay their enlightenment. The Buddha's number-one priority was to lead men to enlightenment by expanding and protecting the sangha. He made a conscious, business decision early in his ministry to bar women from the Order. His common-sense reason was: Putting men and women near each other is just asking for trouble. The events leading to women joining the sangha, in which Ananda was instrumental, is a fascinating insight into human behavior.

The Buddha's choice of Ananda to be his attendant created major personnel problems in the sangha. Many advanced arhats viewed Ananda with suspicion and contempt. When the Buddha's parinirvanization left Ananda without a protector, several senior monks even tried to organize other arhats to prevent Ananda from attending the first council. They criticized many of his decisions and actions in representing the Buddha as wrong and unBuddhist, ostensibly because he was not enlightened. However, mere cursory examination of these passive-aggressive, often underhanded, attempts by Ananda's rivals to exclude him from the first council, reveals the accusations and accusers as more-than-likely the unenlightened ones, not Ananda.

Ananda was recognized even by his opponents as having an encyclopedic knowledge of the Buddha's discourses. Their complaints about Ananda might have stemmed from their own fear-based feelings of inadequacy. As he did during the twenty-five years he served the Buddha, Ananda's measured, calm reply--- I am as one who is still learning---to these serious charges left the arhats sidetracked and confused. How could his interrogators pick that answer apart? Even arhats are still perfecting their enlightenment. Isn't everyone still learning?

The Buddha was a prophet, a brilliant philosopher, and an intriguing person. His long-time attendant, Ananda, is an equally compelling figure, for diametrically different reasons. The Buddha achieved enlightenment by extinguishing the flames of desire. Ananda, however, was not enlightened for the entire twenty-five years he was the Buddha's attendant. It is astounding to realize that the person who was the closest advisor to the first and only enlightened Buddha for our lifetime was not enlightened. This begs the question: Why did the Buddha choose Ananda as his companion and chronicler, rather than numerous enlightened disciples who actively campaigned for the position? I hope to shed some light and provoke some discussion on that issue.

I use a relaxed, conversational writing style to attract general audiences who might have an interest in Buddhism. And since management and motivation is my academic specialty, business leaders might enjoy a character study of Ananda, who became a powerful chief-of-staff effectively serving the Buddha, a brilliant leader who could be irascible and difficult and demanding in his interpersonal relationships. Experienced Buddhist practitioners might also find this examination of Ananda's contributions useful.

This book is my perception of Ananda, the Buddha, the other disciples, and the events surrounding Ananda's life. No one was closer to the Buddha than Ananda. Ananda was there when history was being made. His words and his interactions with the Buddha illuminate the entire early Buddhist movement. Ananda heard, memorized, and recited most of the Buddha's discourses. It is not an exaggeration to say that Buddhism has survived and flourished because of Ananda's selfless dedication.

I hope this biography of Ananda will be a gentle introduction to Buddhism. Too often, people learn about Buddhism through its most complicated principles: rebirth, samsara, dependent arising, emptiness, and mindfulness. This is equivalent to introducing someone to Christianity by trying to explain the Trinity. It's much too complicated. Most people just want to know how any religion can help them be a better person and have happy, fulfilling lives. The Buddha often refused to answer convoluted philosophical questions by responding: "Knowing the answer to this question will not help you in your quest for enlightenment. You should concentrate on the goal." Starting with the benefits certainly makes more sense than a difficult trek into the theological jungle.

I was attracted to Buddhism because each person is responsible for achieving his/her own enlightenment. Belief in a specific person or deity to become enlightened is not required or necessary. Living a moral, ethical life is necessary; and we have the Noble Eightfold Path to help us. The Buddha, his disciples, and the householders who followed him, were all humans who were struggling. The Buddha identified exactly why we suffer and then developed a path to take us out of the repeating cycle of suffering. Those are the benefits of Buddhism that people need to know up-front. The deeper understanding will naturally occur later, after further study.

1

Ananda's Early Life

Ananda's life revolved around the Buddha; so, a brief lineage of the Buddha might be helpful in analyzing the future relationship between the two. Before he became the Buddha, he was born Siddhartha Gautama around 563 BCE in Kapilavatthu. Siddhartha's father, King Suddhodana, was leader of the Sakya clan in the state of Kosala, on the northern border of ancient India. Suddhodana is sometimes described as a hereditary monarch, but modern historians think he was probably an elected head of a tribal confederacy. Whatever his title, Siddhartha's father was very powerful and very rich.

Polygamy was common in that period and King Suddhodana had a large harem of wives and consorts, including his cousin, Maya, who was Siddhartha's mother. Just one week after she gave birth to Siddhartha, Maya died and the King took Maya's younger sister, Prajapati, also a member of his harem, as his wife. Coincidentally, on the same day Maya died, Prajapati gave birth to another child for the King; a son they named Nanda. Siddhartha now had a stepbrother. Prajapati raised Siddhartha as her own son.

Ananda was born around thirty years after Siddhartha, in 593 BCE, in Kapilavatthu, in northeastern India, near what is now the Kingdom of Tibet. Tradition holds that he had spent his previous life as a god in the Tusita heaven.[4]Ananda" is translated as "great delight"[5]or "Joy"[6]

Since Ananda's father, Suklodana, was the younger brother of Siddhartha's father, Ananda and Siddhartha were first cousins. Some sources claim Ananda and the Buddha were the same age and were born on the same day. [7]It is possible that Ananda was born on the same day and, perhaps, even the same month as the Buddha; but the same year is not likely since the evidence is overwhelming that Ananda was much younger than the Buddha.

When Ananda "was in his twenties, the Buddha was 53" [8]"In the Book of the Discipline of the Mulasarvastivadins, he [Ananda] is portrayed as being the same age as the Buddha's son, Rahula, something that makes better sense in view of his later roles"[9]After Buddha delivered a discourse to Ananda and a gathering of monks, Ananda began his reply by stating that he was Buddha's "youngest relative" [10]

Ananda grew up hearing stories about the exploits of his famous cousin. The early sangha was a family affair. In the second year of his ministry, The Buddha returned to his hometown of Kapilavatthu and personally ordained Ananda[11]along with seven princes of the Sakya clan. Ananda was the youngest of the group [12]Ananda was also the cousin of Anuradha, another of the Buddha's great disciples. Ananda and Anuradha became monks at the same time. Ananda and his older brother, Devadatta,[13]also a disciple of the Buddha, had totally different personalities and motivations. Ananda was pious and studious. Devadatta constantly tried to disrupt the sangha with unwise policy recommendations and clumsy attempts to wrest control of the sangha away from the Buddha. Several times, Devadatta tried to murder the Buddha.

The Buddha had the thirty-two signs that marked him "as having attained complete Buddhahood; but Ananda lacked one of the thirty-two, which caused him trouble." [14]The marks of a buddha are physical attributes considered desirable for a buddha or a great man. The missing mark that prevented Ananda from being born a buddha has never been identified. Clearly, Ananda's difficulty in regulating his interpersonal relationships with females was a klesha that could have contributed to his inability to achieve enlightenment during the Buddha's life. Unfortunately, there are no psychological or emotional attributes of a buddha that would address that issue.

Buddhists believe that this is not our first rodeo. We all have past lives, probably many thousands of rebirths. This samsara, the cycle of birth-death-rebirth, is a core principle of Buddhism. The Buddha and Ananda had many thousands of past lives over millennia. Ananda's previous lives were a training ground for his later position as the Buddha's caregiver and confidant. "In Ananda's past lives, he was seldom a god, unlike his stepbrother Anuruddha and seldom an animal, unlike his cousin Devadatta."[15] In his former lives, Ananda frequently had a connection somehow with a Buddha, as father, son, brother, assistant, colleague, or friend. The threads that would later connect Ananda and the Buddha in their remarkable friendship and collaboration were evident. In the following past-life accounts, the names "Ananda" and "Siddhartha" are used to distinguish the two and to keep the characters separated, although, of course, both had not yet reached their ultimate rebirths.

In a previous life, Ananda and Siddhartha were Candalas, of the lowest caste. Since they were outcasts, they had the worst jobs imaginable: cleaning "malodorous places." To escape their awful existence, they disguised themselves as Brahmin and surreptitiously attended a university. Other students discovered their subterfuge and attacked them. A wise and kindly man stopped the beat-down and counseled them. Both took his advice and become ascetics. When they died, they were reborn as animals, the offspring of a doe, as punishment for their deceit. They were both killed by a hunter. In the next life, they were both reborn as sea hawks and, again, were killed by a hunter.

Their rebirths as sea hawks exhausted the negative karma, so in the next life, Ananda was reborn as the son of a king and Siddhartha as the son of a chaplain. Siddhartha was extremely spiritual and became Ananda's mentor. He counseled Ananda on the futility of the world of the senses and praised the ascetic life. Ananda said he understood what Siddhartha was saying but, in a revealing statement that foreshadowed problems in his future rebirth, Ananda said he felt trapped by his desires, held motionless, "like an elephant in a swamp." Siddhartha reassured Ananda that he could still practice virtue as king, for example, by not severely taxing his subjects and by supporting priests and ascetics. And, if those pesky feelings of desire occurred again, Siddhartha suggested that Ananda think about his mother and how she had protected him when he was a helpless baby.

In a different past life, Siddhartha was a king, Ananda a poor watercarrier. In a wonderful parable, Ananda's only possession was a coin that he kept hidden under a rock, twelve miles away. A festival was being held in the city and his wife suggested he get his coin and she would match it. Then, they could go to the festival and really celebrate. In a chipper mood, Ananda headed off in the boiling noon-day sun to get the coin and was happily singing when the king heard him and asked why he was so joyous.

When Ananda told him, the king said he would give him a coin, so he would not have to walk in the scorching sun. Ananda accepted the king's offer and remarked that when he retrieved his coin and added it to his wife's coin and the king's contribution, he and his wife could really have a good time at the festival. The king kept offering money to Ananda to keep him out of the sun, but Ananda still insisted on getting his own coin from beneath the rock.

The king kept raising the offer and Ananda kept refusing until, finally, in desperation, the king offered Ananda half of his kingdom, if Ananda would just use some common sense and stay in the shade. Ananda agreed and was thereafter known as King One-Coin. In this story, Ananda exhibited the persuasive abilities and tactical shrewdness that he would use very effectively when he was fending off critics in a later rebirth as the Buddha's attendant.

But the story didn't end there. The two kings went hunting one day and stopped to rest. Siddhartha put his head in Ananda's lap and fell asleep. The thought came to Ananda: if he killed the king, he would have the whole kingdom to himself. Ananda was slowly drawing his sword to slay the king when he remembered how kind and helpful the king had been to him; so, he sheathed his sword.

But the murderous thoughts kept plaguing him. Finally, Ananda threw his sword away, awakened the king, and asked for his forgiveness. The king not only forgave Ananda but offered Ananda his entire kingdom. The king even said he would work for Ananda as his viceroy. This might seem a surprising reaction to a person who admits that he thought about cutting your throat as you slept; but, since the king would later become the Buddha, it was not surprising at all. Ananda declined the offer, saying his lust for power was over. He became an ascetic.

In a different past life, Siddhartha was King of Benares. He was gentle and righteous. One of his ministers "carried on an intrigue in his harem," and the penalty for that crime was usually death, but rather than execute the minister, Siddhartha banished him and his family. The minister moved to a nearby kingdom, which happened to be the court of King Ananda. To ingratiate himself with King Ananda, the minister gossiped that King Siddhartha was feckless, a push-over, and King Ananda could easily occupy Benares.

King Ananda was suspicious, but the minister suggested an experiment, of sorts, by invading a village in the Benares kingdom. He predicted that, if any of the marauders were captured, the weak King Siddhartha would probably just reward the prisoners. The plan was set in motion. The raiders were indeed captured, and they told King Siddhartha that they had plundered the village only because they had no food and were starving. Instead of a sword to the neck, King Siddhartha gave them money. This convinced King Ananda that the minister's predictions were accurate, so he invaded Benares.

Against the advice of his military experts, King Siddhartha refused to defend the city, saying he did not want to harm others. Besides, he said, if King Ananda wanted Benares that badly, he could have it. King Siddhartha even allowed King Ananda to capture him. While imprisoned, King Siddhartha practiced loving-kindness meditation toward King Ananda, who developed a fever and suffered greatly from a guilty conscience.

He asked King Siddhartha for his pardon and returned Siddhartha's kingdom to him. King Siddhartha told his ministers about the many lives he had saved by his nonviolent reaction to King Ananda's aggression.

Both kings showed glimpses of their future lives. Siddhartha gave up his throne and became an ascetic, which is perfectly in step with the future Buddha. And Ananda didn't give up anything. He continued as King, which is also consistent with his later attachments with the physical/sensual world as the Buddha's attendant.

2

Formation of the Sangha

Early in the Buddha's ministry, Sariputra, a Brahman of the highest caste, brought five hundred of his disciples, all great scholars, to debate and, Sariputra hoped, defeat the Buddha. Sariputra intended to convert the Buddha to their beliefs. But after only a few moments of discussion, the Buddha boldly challenged Sariputra: "One thing is certain. You cannot convert me. The only possibility is that you will be converted, so think twice"[16] Wonderful chutzpah! The Buddha trash-talking a competitor!

Sariputra did not have to think twice. The Buddha's brilliance was obvious. Sariputra "was already converted." He said, "I know that neither can I argue now, nor will I be able to argue then. You have finished my argumentation. Now I cannot argue because I don't have eyes; then I will not be able to argue because I have eyes. But I am going to stay."[17] Sariputra told his disciples, "Now I am no longer your master; Here is the man. I will be sitting by his side as his disciple. Please forget me as your master. If you want to be here, he is your master now"[18] The Buddha's sangha, translated as community, immediately gained five hundred new initiates.

The Buddha required his disciples to be single, male, and celibate. Married men with families (householders/lay people) were not allowed to join the sangha because they brought spouses and children and all their problems. But the Buddha made it possible for householders to take refuge in the Buddha, Dharma, and sangha. This allowed non-monks to become involved with Buddhist principles and certainly promoted good will from the community toward Buddhism. But householders could not seek enlightenment.

The Buddha was steadfastly opposed to women in the sangha. They presented an entirely different, complicated set of problems. From a purely managerial standpoint, it was cheaper and more efficient to provide food and lodging for a group of single, celibate Bhikshus, who could be housed in large, open dormitories.

The Buddha was a man of his times. He lived in India during the Axial Age, which had a paternalistic power structure operating within a strict hierarchy of social castes. He grew up with men totally in charge and that's the way he ran his sangha. However, even in this oppressive environment for females and lower-caste men, the Buddha transcended many of the prevailing prejudices. Today, the Buddha could be considered progressive because he did not consider social caste when admitting men to the sangha and he eventually even admitted women to the Order, albeit with many restrictions.

Although the Buddha's fame as a seer and teacher brought many new converts to the Order, it also brought the organizational and managerial problems that are present in any large company. The Buddha now had to deal with power struggles, turf wars, and personality clashes among his disciples. The sangha was composed of

- senior, enlightened disciples whom the Buddha had chosen and nurtured.
- dedicated mid-level monks who accepted the Four Noble Truths and carefully followed the Noble Eightfold Path in their quest for enlightenment.
- new converts who worked studiously to learn the Buddha's discourses but were far from enlightenment and needed constant instruction and guidance from senior monks.
- wanderers who were searching for answers.

- adventurers who were simply along for the ride and a free meal.
- members of lower castes who viewed membership in the sangha as their only realistic opportunity to improve their social standing. The Buddha did not discriminate according to caste or wealth; and seniority was based on when a monk was ordained. For example, an Untouchable who was ordained an hour before a Brahmin would outrank the Brahmin in the sangha. This was a powerful incentive for lower-caste men to become monks.
- and those who saw membership in the sangha not as a path to enlightenment, but to acquire power and prestige.

Into this mix came Ananda. "A gentle, scrupulous man" [19] Ananda's star rose quickly in the sangha due, in large part, to his astonishing ability to accurately memorize and recite the Buddha's discourses and his unfailing loyalty to the Buddha. Since Ananda was not enlightened, he was the subject of much criticism and jealousy from enlightened followers of the Buddha. Nevertheless, over many years, Ananda skillfully created a powerful niche for himself in the sangha hierarchy. Since enlightenment extinguishes all intense desires, the obvious question arises as to whether the senior monks who were jealous of Ananda were truly enlightened.

The Buddha and his disciples were men and women, not deities. In fact, the Buddha never claimed to be a god. To help deal with human emotions, The Buddha urged his disciples to follow the middle way, commonly known as all things in moderation. This core Buddhist tenet is a clear indication that the Buddha never expected disciples to totally extinguish all feelings; to become emotionless androids. Only desires and attachments at the far end of the scale, such as extreme hatred or possessive love, are destructive. The Buddha urged steady, mindful progress toward enlightenment.

Acceptance of the Buddha's teachings grew quickly, and the sangha membership increased accordingly. The exact number of initiates, monks, and nuns in the Order is difficult to estimate; but the small group of five aesthetics the Buddha converted immediately after his enlightenment grew rapidly into a large sangha through the years. Early in Buddha's ministry, Upatissa, who would become one of Buddha's most eminent disciples, joined the sangha and brought two hundred converts[20]

Several years later, a king observing a well-disciplined assembly of monks remarked incredulously: "You are playing me no tricks? How can it be that there should be no sound at all, not a sneeze, not a cough, in so large an Assembly, among one thousand two hundred fifty of the brethren?"[21]There is no doubt that the sangha was quickly expanding its membership and that would bring problems.

Later, chroniclers described a multitude of monks, nuns, and laypeople gathered to listen to the Buddha's discourses. Multitude cannot be translated into an exact figure, but writers in the Axial Age seemed to consider any big crowd of people a multitude. However, when describing Ananda's past lives, it is recorded that Buddha Padumuttara, who existed "one hundred thousand aeons ago" once had a "retinue of one hundred thousand monks."[22]It is also recorded that "a community of 700,000 monks" had come together for the Buddha's funeral [23]Regardless of the exact figure, the sangha had grown immensely from the five original ascetic converts to thousands. The Buddha needed someone to schedule his activities---a chief-of-staff.

It is important to remember that nothing was written down during this period in history. The Buddha and Ananda came from prosperous families in the warrior caste, near the top of Indian society, so it is possible that they could read and write, but there is no indication in the records one way or the other. Even if the Buddha and Ananda were literate, most of their disciples were not, which required that all the Buddha's directives and sermons be spoken, closely listened to, memorized exactly, and then accurately transmitted, orally, to other monks and lay people.

Since there was no written policy book or The Buddha's Rules of Order to settle disagreements, the Buddha spent much of his time putting out fires and settling disagreements among his followers. Ananda was the Buddha's personal envoy or ambassador, a walking tape recorder. If the Buddha told Ananda to take a message to a group of monks in a nearby village, it was vital that Ananda get the message right by faithfully transmitting the actual words and subtle meanings intended by the Buddha.

As the sangha's membership increased, so did the need for better organization of the Dharma (the Buddha's discourses) and Vinaya (monastic rules). "It is said that in the early days of the sangha in India no rules were necessary because all the members of the sangha were destined for nirvana and their behaviour was, therefore, naturally correct. It was only when the sangha grew that the Buddha decided it was necessary to establish a monastic code."[24]

To meet the increasing public demand for the Buddha's discourses, a system was established to organize and disseminate the Buddha's teachings. The process was simple and intuitive. Individual monks chose areas of specialization, such as recitation of Sutras or rules of discipline and doctrinal aspects of the monastic code, and other important elements of the burgeoning spiritual movement. Ananda quickly distinguished himself among the disciples and impressed the Buddha with his amazing ability to memorize and accurately repeat entire Sutras, which was so important in the dissemination of the Buddha's teachings. Ananda soon became a "suttantika, a master of the discourses" [25]

The exacting nature of Ananda's duties must have been extremely stressful and nerve-wracking, but Ananda became a human repository for all the Buddha's sermons for the last twenty-five years of the Buddha's life. That oral system of transmission was used for several centuries until around 100 B.C.E., when the Buddha's discourses were written down, in the Pali language, on palm leaves and stored in baskets.[26]

Ananda's pleasant personality "attracted others and commanded their respect." [27]He skillfully navigated the treacherous waters of Sangha politics, while building his reputation as an excellent hearer of the Buddha's discourses. He did not let his rivals' attempts to damage his influence with the Buddha due to his non-enlightenment affect his ability to serve the Buddha and when the opportunity for advancement presented itself, Ananda was ready.

3

Ananda is Promoted

For the first twenty-five years after the Buddha's enlightenment, he did not have a full-time attendant. Monks with specific skills helped him with various sangha functions, but it was an unofficial, ad-hoc arrangement.[28]Apparently, the Buddha was not satisfied with any of his part-time attendants. The Buddha complained that "sometimes his attendants would not obey him, and on certain occasions had dropped his bowl and robe and gone away, leaving him."[29] He "desired to have somebody as his permanent body-servant, one who would respect his wishes in every way." [30]

At the age of fifty-five[31]his twenty-fifth year of constant traveling to teach the dharma, the Buddha was physically worn out. In one of his discourses, he told his followers: "I am now getting old, my body is growing infirm, and my life draws near to the end of its day. I must have a personal attendant. Choose me one and let him look after my wants, and let him, more carefully than any, remember my words as I teach you."[32]

Thousands of disciples were working toward enlightenment and the Buddha preached the dharma for almost forty-four years, but it is estimated that only "about two dozen people became enlightened."[33]There is no estimate of the number of enlightened disciples at the Buddha's twenty-five-year mark, but it appears that every arhat, who must be enlightened to earn that title, enthusiastically applied for the position. The Buddha rejected all of them, ostensibly due to their advanced age.[34]

Once again, the versions of events differ slightly. In one, Maha-maudgalyayana, one of the Buddha's ten major disciples, realized that the Buddha had already decided who he wanted for his attendant. Maha-maudgalyayana meditated deeply and used his inner vision to conclude that the Buddha wanted Ananda. He and a group of monks went to Ananda's cell and asked him to become the Buddha's attendant.

In another version, Ananda is standing silently in the background as arhats eagerly volunteer and are all rejected by the Buddha. When asked by a monk why he didn't seek the job, Ananda responded that the Buddha knew exactly whom he wanted as his attendant. And Ananda was right. The Buddha told the gathering: "Among my disciples there is one who is the most frequent hearer, remembers all my teachings, has no questions on any point, and knows why I told each particular truth and when and where. This disciple is Ananda."[35]

This incident epitomized Ananda's keen understanding the power dynamics of the sangha as well as the Buddha's thought process. Ananda had been quietly building a relationship of trust with the Buddha over many years. The ambitious monks scrambled for position, but, in a brilliant strategic move, Ananda hung back and waited for the seeds of trust he planted in the Buddha to ripen.

All the descriptions of the important conversation between Ananda and the Buddha prior to Ananda's appointment as the Buddha's attendant indicate that Ananda did not immediately accept the Buddha's offer. It seems impossible to imagine that a disciple would negotiate his job duties with the Buddha, but Ananda did. In one, version, Ananda said he would accept the position if the Buddha agreed to the following requests: (1) that Ananda would never wear the robe of the Buddha, whether old or new; (2) that Ananda would never eat food prepared especially for the Buddha; and (3) that Ananda would not attend to the Buddha except at prescribed times.

In version two, Ananda asked that (1) he not receive any material benefits from serving the Buddha; (2) he be allowed to vet and schedule visitors to the Buddha; (3) he be allowed to ask questions about the Buddha's discourses and (4) the Buddha would repeat any teachings that Ananda had missed.

In version 3, Ananda asks that the Buddha (1) never give him any choice food or garment gotten by him; (2) nor appoint for him a separate "fragrant cell;"(3) nor include him in the invitations accepted by the Buddha; (4) allow him to accept invitations on behalf of the Buddha; (5) allow him to bring to the Buddha those who came to see him from afar; (6) allow him to place before the Buddha all his perplexities; (7) and the Buddha was to repeat to him any doctrine taught in his absence. Ananda said those privileges would allow monks to trust him because the Buddha trusted him. Ananda concluded by saying "if these concessions were not granted, some would ask where was the advantage of such service."[36]

This was a bold move by Ananda. The organizational skills he later exhibited in serving the Buddha were on full display here. Although his title was attendant, he had created the world's first chief-of-staff position. He had true power because he controlled access to the leader.

These three accounts are similar in content. They concentrate on the public image of Ananda as the dedicated servant who seeks no personal material gain from the Buddha. Ananda knew his requests would dispel possible concerns by the Sangha that he had ulterior motives for seeking to be the Buddha's attendant. Ananda wanted to make it clear that he took the job only to truly serve the Buddha, not to get better food, more food, fancy robes, a nicer cell, or other perks. This would help Ananda gain the trust of the Sangha. Ironically, Ananda's promise that he would not eat any food prepared specially for the Buddha turned out later to be a tragic mistake.

In yet another version, in a masterful display of courage, Ananda brazenly informed the Buddha that after he is ordained, Ananda will be the Buddha's disciple and will be required to follow the Buddha's orders. But for now, the Buddha must do what Ananda asks because Ananda is the Buddha's elder cousin. The Buddha replies, "I know you. You cannot ask anything that will put your younger cousin in any difficulty. You can ask."

Ananda requested that (1) before the Buddha went to sleep at night, he answers any questions Ananda had. Ananda promised not to disturb the Buddha during the day, "but I am a human being and I am not enlightened; certain questions may arise;" (2) "You will never tell me to go anywhere else; I will always be with you, to serve you till my last breath. You will not tell me, 'Now you go and spread my message,' the way you send others. You cannot send me;" (3) "If I ask you to give some time to somebody, at any hour, it may be an odd hour, in the middle of the night, you will have to meet the person. That much privilege you have to give me."[37]

This account of Ananda's requests differs from others when Ananda is described as older than the Buddha, Ananda's demands to the Buddha seem demanding. The entire premise of Ananda, the elder, giving directives to the Buddha, the younger, is jolting and does not fit reports of Ananda's consistently respectful behavior toward the Buddha. Besides, the prevailing evidence indicates that Ananda was at least thirty years younger than the Buddha, which better explains the relationship between the two.

It is interesting, however, in his first demand, Ananda admits his lack of enlightenment might require the Buddha to extend and amplify certain teachings. The Buddha followed through with Ananda's second demand that he not be sent on missions away from the Buddha to spread the message. Ananda's third demand that he be given total discretion to decide who could see the Buddha at any time, day, or night, was extraordinary. In that simple negotiation, Ananda wrested power away from more senior, enlightened disciples.

The Buddha agreed to Ananda's requests and "when Buddha was fifty-five years old, Ananda was twenty-five and he became the personal attendant of Buddha."[38] In fact, the Buddha officially informed senior disciple Maha-maudgalyayana that Ananda would have important duties: "He will care for and arrange fit times for the Bhiksu and the Bhiksuni to see the Buddha; for the Upasaka and Upasika; for the different scholars of different religions, for the monks of other faiths. He will settle the time when the various scholars of different schools, or the monks of different faiths shall meet in argument with the Buddha."[39]

The Buddha continued, in an eerie harbinger of his own death later: "He will offer only that food to the Buddha which will be best for him. He will know whether certain foods would hinder the Buddha's eloquence in speech or give him more vigor. Isn't it wonderful that he knows so well!"[40]

The Buddha was obviously excited that he finally had found a trustworthy chief-of-staff to systemize his daily activities. He gushed about Ananda's organizational abilities: "O Maudgalyayana, Ananda will perfectly know whether, at the noon time, the Buddha will rise from his seat and talk to all; or on that day will go to a certain place; or on that day will remain quietly in relaxation. He will know everything exactly as I have said, never anything to the contrary. Isn't it wonderful! He is like that."[41]

Ananda's title of attendant to the Buddha did not reflect his actual power and responsibilities. He was the Treasurer/Guardian of the Dispensation. In a political state, the treasurer ensures the state's wealth is protected. The treasurer must be scrupulously honest, reliable, and focused on his job. In a religion, the wealth, the dispensations, are the teachings. And in an oral culture, the ability to accurately hear, memorize, and recite the Buddha's discourses was vital. Ananda's superb memory ensured that his position in the sangha was second only to the Buddha.[42]

To be an attendant for a Buddha, one must first aspire to it and perform "many meritorious deeds over one hundred thousand world cycles."[43] Ananda started his training "one hundred thousand aeons in the past" as a monk named Sumana who was the younger half-brother of Bodhisatta Gotama, who was then known as Jatila. Sumana served Buddha Padumuttara and his sangha of 100,000 monks during the three-month rainy season.[44] Sumana's job was roughly equivalent to an internship or a part-time job. Buddha Padumuttara was so impressed by Sumana's devotion that he told Sumana that his aspiration to serve a Buddha full-time would reach fruition one hundred thousand years in the future with Buddha Gotama.[45] "From this time onwards, Ananda continued to perform meritorious deeds to fulfill his aspiration."[46]

For the next twenty-five years, during the height of the Buddha's ministry, Ananda was the Buddha's constant, trusted companion on most of his travels. Ananda had an extensive job description. He took care of the Buddha's daily needs, which were many and varied: He watched over the Buddha and made sure the Master was rested. He brought drinking water to the Buddha and washed the Buddha's face and feet. He gave the Buddha tooth-wood for cleaning his teeth. He arranged the Buddha's seat. He massaged his back and rubbed his body. He fanned the Buddha, swept his cell, and mended his robes. Ananda carried messages to-and-from the Buddha and the monks. He obtained medicine for the Buddha when he was ailing. "In this way Ananda performed the many daily tasks and cared for the physical well-being of his enlightened cousin like a good mother or a caring wife."[47] Ananda was the archetype of the dedicated chief-of-staff. In fact, "the Buddha described Ananda as a learned, mindful, well-behaved and resolute disciple." [48]

Societal violence and assassinations occurred in antiquity, just as in modern times. The Buddha had become a powerful figure, a moral leader who was disrupting social norms. He allowed lower-caste men, called untouchables, to join the sangha and become an ordained monk, which improved their lives immediately. They did not have to continue to suffer in this life in the belief that, in their next life, they might be reborn into a higher caste. Then, in an even greater revolutionary act, the Buddha allowed women to join the Sangha and to seek enlightenment. Buddhism gave the down-trodden hope; and people with hope can be very frightening to those in power.

Thus, it was imperative that the Buddha be protected. Two attempts to assassinate the Buddha had already been unsuccessful. Moggallana, one of the Buddha's ten most influential disciples, was murdered in a rockslide. Although the Buddha's personal protection was not discussed openly, Ananda became the Buddha's unofficial bodyguard. He accompanied the Buddha wherever he went, "like a shadow that does not depart."[49] and ensured that the sangha's campgrounds were safe. He slept near the Buddha and "...guarded the Buddha's cell at night. Carrying a staff and a torch, "he would go nine times around the Buddha's Gandha-kuti in order to keep awake, in case he were needed, and also to prevent the Buddha's sleep from being disturbed."[50] This little-known, but very important, duty to guard the Buddha might explain the zeal with which Ananda vetted the Buddha's visitors. The staff Ananda carried was not for show. He was prepared to use it to defend the Buddha from marauding animals and equally dangerous men.

Ananda's most influential and powerful administrative function was controlling access to the Buddha. Today, Ananda might be described as the Buddha's chief-of-staff. Even monks who were enlightened and senior to Ananda had to ask him for permission to talk with the Buddha. This must have rankled the arhats and led to increasing tension between Ananda and the arhats.

Ananda was the first person the Buddha called for help. In one case, a Bhikkhu had a severe case of dysentery and was lying in his own filth. None of the other monks would help him. The Buddha, assisted by Ananda, washed the man, and put him on a clean bed.[51] In a different incident, a monk at the Jetavana monastery was covered in painful boils, which constantly burst, staining his robes, and emitting a horrible smell. Eventually, his fellow monks could not take it anymore. They carried the monk outside to an open field and left him. Once again, the Buddha and Ananda took care of the suffering monk. This time, however, the other monks, inspired by the Buddha and Ananda, prepared hot water, washed the ailing monk's robes, and tried to make him comfortable.[52]

Ananda became a force to be reckoned with. It didn't take long for monks to conclude that the insignificant-sounding title of attendant, did not accurately describe the enormous power Ananda wielded. Although not in a powerful position himself, he exerted power because he was always close to the power and had the ear of the leader. And, most importantly, by vetting who could meet personally with the Buddha, Ananda was able to exert control over more senior monks.

Ananda is usually recognized for two major achievements: He

persuaded the Buddha to allow women to join the sangha although Buddhist scholars say it is impossible to persuade or influence a Buddha about anything and he planted a tree; but it had more significance than just a tree.

The home-base for the Buddha and his sangha was Jetavana monastery, near the ancient city of Sravasti, present-day Uttar Pradesh. The Buddha spent a lot of time traveling from village to village, teaching the dharma. Pilgrims and visitors, who often came long distances to Sravasti to pay their respects to the Buddha and to hear his Sutras, were very disappointed if the Buddha was gone.

Ananda recognized, in modern terms, a public relations problem. They needed something to pacify the disappointed pilgrims. Not surprisingly, the Buddha had the answer. He told Ananda to go to Bodh Gaya and get a sapling from the Bodhi Tree under which the Buddha had gained enlightenment. Then, Ananda was to plant the tree in front of the gateway of Jetavana monastery. "In my absence let my devotees pay homage to the great Bodhi Tree that gave me protection during enlightenment. Let the Bodhi Tree be a symbol of my presence. Those who honour the Bodhi Tree would in essence be honouring and paying homage to me."[53]

Of course, Ananda accomplished this goal. It is important to note that the Buddha trusted Ananda with this important mission, even though it was shortly after Ananda was appointed as the Buddha's attendant. Since the tree was planted under Ananda's direction, it came to be known as the AnandaBodhi Tree.

Ananda was the Buddha's confidant and, as indicated by the records, probably the Buddha's best friend; although neither would describe their relationship with those words, since any strong attachment to anyone or anything is detrimental to becoming enlightened. It is clear, however, that the Buddha had a strong fondness for Ananda. The Buddha praised Ananda's devotion: "Your acts of love and kindness have been invariable and are beyond measure.[54] Ananda was so devoted to the Buddha that "when the Buddha was ill, Ananda became sympathetically sick."[55] The Buddha's intense mindfulness and concentration allowed him to regulate his love for Ananda, so it would not reach the destructive level of an attachment.

Ananda used his position as the Buddha's chief-of-staff to protect the Buddha from frivolous requests. Sometimes "too pious admirers… tried to persuade the Buddha to do what was against his scruples" In what had to be one of the tackiest requests Ananda received, a rich man "asked the Buddha to walk over the carpets in his mansion."[56]The stated purpose is not clear but, presumably, the Buddha's tracks would bless the carpet. Whether the Buddha did it is not recorded.

The Buddha had immense respect for Ananda, personally and professionally. When the Buddha wanted an important principle to be remembered, he told Ananda. Ananda was present for almost all the Buddha's major discourses and remembered all of them. When teaching, the Buddha would often say something enigmatic or ambiguous and then leave, forcing the monks to talk about it and, hopefully, arrive at the correct understanding. The Buddha's mastery as a teacher is revealed by this technique. Sometimes, we learn more when we must work to achieve the answer, rather than having the teacher tell us.

The monks, like students today, sometimes did not want to struggle with the difficult concepts, so they would often ask Ananda to explain the Buddha's statements. When the Buddha was told about Ananda's interpretation of his words, the Buddha replied: "Ananda, monks, is wise, one of great understanding. If you had questioned me about this matter, I would have answered in the very same way that Ananda has answered. That is the meaning, and so you should bear it in mind"[57]It is high praise for someone who is not enlightened to answer complicated questions of theology spoken by the Master.

In one case, King Pasenadi of Kosala met with Ananda and asked him a series of questions "about the criteria of proper conduct in body, speech, and mind." [58]The King was so impressed by Ananda's answers that he effusively praised Ananda to the Buddha:

> Lord, what is the name of this monk?
> His name is Ananda (Joy) great king.
> What a joy he is! What a true joy!... [59]

The King also gave Ananda a costly garment. As per his agreement with the Buddha, Ananda reported the meeting and gift to the Buddha and, presumably, gave the article of clothing to the Buddha, who praised Ananda before an assembly of monks: "It is a gain for King Pasenadi of Kosala, monks, it is fortunate for King Pasenadi of Kosala that he gained the opportunity to see Ananda and to offer him service." [60]

Ananda's fame as a skilled teacher was put to the test by the monk Channa, who was Prince Siddhartha's royal charioteer earlier in their lives. Channa later became an ordained monk and joined the sangha. He never missed an opportunity to boast that it was he who showed Prince Siddhartha the four sights that propelled Siddhartha toward enlightenment. His overbearing and obnoxious behavior alienated other monks. But he really touched the third rail when he unwisely criticized Sariputra and Moggallana, the Buddha's chief two disciples. Channa earned the unenviable reputation as "an obdurate bhikkhu, self-willed and difficult to train."[61]

His advancement was stalled because he feared nirvana would destroy his ego, which, of course, it would. Channa was caught in a samsara-like haze, in which he recognized his huge attachment to his ego, and he knew how to extinguish it, but he could not give it up. He kept repeating the same behaviors. Finally, though, Channa realized that, despite his past relationship with the Buddha, his days as a monk were numbered unless he reined in his out-of-control ego. He humbly asked Ananda for help. Channa listened carefully as Ananda recited one of the Buddha's sermons. Ananda's explanation was so effective that Channa "became securely established in the Dhamma." [62]and started on the path of enlightenment as a stream-enterer.

Although the Buddha and Ananda continued to counsel Channa, his arrogance caused so many problems in the sangha that, on his deathbed, the Buddha ordered the other monks to not speak to Channa until he repented his awful behavior.[63]Channa found out about the Buddha's decree and fainted...three times. Then, full of remorse, he asked the assembly to pardon him for his actions. He received his pardon and eventually became an arhat.

Ananda was a gifted teacher of the Dhamma; but even he could not reach a zealous lay disciple named Atula and a group of his friends when they visited the Jetavana monastery to take in a discourse. First, they approached the monk Revata, "who was a solitary, contemplative type and had nothing to say to them." Then, they found Sariputra the Buddha's chief disciple. Sariputra loved to talk and happily began a long, detailed discourse on philosophy; but they found his sermon "abstruse and tedious."

As the group wandered through the monastery, they ran across Ananda and vented their frustrations concerning Revata and Sariputra. Ananda was very skilled at translating difficult principles into terms that lay disciples could understand; so, he gave a discourse "expressed in simple language." The group was still not impressed and complained to the Buddha. Atula and his friends clearly did not or could not understand Buddhist doctrine; even when Ananda took it down to a basic level; but the Buddha quietly and respectfully listened to their uninformed critiques of Sariputra and Ananda. His response was a priceless combination of weariness, frustration, disappointment, and resignation:

> Throughout history it has been the practice of men to
> criticize other men. A man who says nothing is liable
> to be criticized, as a man who says a great deal or a man
> who says neither too little nor too much. Everyone comes
> in for blame, as well as praise; even kings do. The
> great earth, the sun, the moon, I myself sitting and
> speaking in the assembly, are criticized by some
> and praised by others. But praise and blame bestowed
> idly are of no account. It is the praise or blame of the
> truly discerning man that matters. [64]

One can imagine the blank stares directed at the Buddha when he finished his response. It is doubtful that Atula and his rowdy group understood the Buddha's subtle message that, since they were clearly not discerning men, their opinion did not matter.

An exciting revelation that emerged in researching this project was the constancy of human reactions, despite disparate cultures and across thousands of years. Human nature has not changed. The Buddha, his disciples, and the local community, struggled with the same problems that we deal with today. For example, two and a half millennia ago, some people wanted a quick fix. They expected learning to be easy and, of course, fun. But most things worth learning, then and now, are not always easy and often, not a lot of fun. Learning requires hard work.

The Buddha's inner circle was composed of bhikkhus who were experts in one or two areas of the Dharma. Ananda was described as "a favorite disciple of the Buddha"[65] and the only disciple whom the Buddha declared was "foremost in five categories:"

- of those who had "heard much/learned much" of the Buddha's discourses.
- of those who had a good memory.
- of those who had mastery of over the sequential structure of the teachings.
- of those who were steadfast in study.
- of the Buddha's attendants.[66]

Ananda's amazing mindfulness gave him the ability to remember and accurately recite The Buddha's sermons "up to sixty-thousand words, without leaving out a single syllable."[67] His phenomenal memory allowed him to remember and flawlessly repeat "fifteen thousand four-line stanzas of the Buddha."[68]

Since Ananda was usually at the Buddha's side when the Master delivered his Sutras, the Buddha would often ask Ananda questions in front of the assembled monks to illustrate specific points. Thus, many of the reported conversations between the Buddha and Ananda are teachings delivered by the Buddha in a question/answer format. Ananda served an important role as an interlocutor.[69] He asked questions that might be obvious to an enlightened arhat but were difficult for unenlightened monks or laypersons. For example, Ananda once asked the Buddha a straight-forward, honest question: "how can one live happily in the Order? "The Buddha's answer was equally direct: be virtuous and don't blame others for their lack of virtue; watch yourself, not others; don't seek fame; obtain the four meditative absorptions; and become an arahant.[70]

On another occasion, Ananda asked "whether there was a fragrance that went against the wind, different from that of flowers and blossoms." The Buddha's reply? "The fragrance of one who has taken the Triple Refuge and who is virtuous and generous." [71]

Ananda was the Buddha's representative for the unenlightened. The Buddha and his arhats had cleansed themselves of intense desires and emotions, so the Buddha needed someone to remind him of the difficulties encountered by unenlightened monks. Ananda fit the bill nicely. Ananda was everymonk. Ananda's emotional reactions and, frankly, his lack of understanding of some key Buddhist principles, helped the Buddha gauge the effectiveness of his discourses. If Ananda had a question, the Buddha could assume that many of the unenlightened listeners and novice monks had the same question. In that sense, Ananda was a valuable member of the Buddha's inner circle.

Ananda once remarked to the Buddha that, "it seems to me, Lord, that good friendship is half of the holy life." The Buddha disagreed: "Do not speak thus, Ananda! Noble friendship is more than half the holy life. It is the entire holy life."[72] The Buddha understood that, for any organization to be successful, its members must feel they are an integral part of the overall effort. Friendship, acceptance, and mentorship are very important.

This is a good place to dispel a common misunderstanding that enlightenment eliminates all desires and emotions. It does not. If the Noble Eightfold Path is followed correctly, one learns the proper emphasis for all thoughts, feelings, and actions is the middle way. Extremes are to be avoided. Gluttony is the opposite of extreme fasting. Both are equally harmful. The Buddha never required believers to not care about another person. Desires only became dangerous when they became obsessive.

However, there is a huge practical caveat that must be considered.

Adhering to the middle way outside of a strictly regulated monastery can be very difficult. Therefore, monks had to be single and celibate. The romantic, sexual desire for a spouse, often resulting in children, might be the foundation of society, but it is detrimental to breaking the fetters that keep us chained to samsara. The Buddha was once Prince Siddhartha---a man who loved his wife. When he left the sleeping Yasodhara and newborn son Rahula, in the middle of the night, to seek enlightenment, he did not wake them because he feared his wife's emotional pleas might cause him to hesitate or reconsider his decision. This is a powerful illustration that Siddhartha, who had laser focus and determination throughout his life, had to struggle with the extreme guilt he felt by leaving his family. His very human indecision and hurt is easily understood by everyone in every generation.

Ananda once witnessed an archer do some amazing shots. Since the Buddha and Ananda both came from the warrior caste, Ananda excitedly recounted what he saw to the Buddha. By using a simple analogy, the Master said it was "more difficult to understand and penetrate the Four Noble Truths than to hit and penetrate with an arrow a hair split seven times."[73] This is an example of Ananda seeing the world through unenlightened eyes; while the Buddha used Ananda's observations to drive home an important theological point.

The Buddha's and Ananda's relatives, the Sakya clan, were opening a new rest house. The Buddha and the monks were invited to spend the night there to bless the dwelling. After speaking for much of the night, the Buddha, in physical distress, turned to Ananda: "Speak to the Sakyas, Ananda, about the disciple in higher training who is practicing the path. My back is aching, and I need to stretch myself." [74]

Once again, the Buddha reveals his humanity. He is not a god. He never claimed to be a god. He is a man, albeit a very special man. He is enlightened. He has discovered how to end suffering for everyone forever. But he is still a man. And now this enlightened man has a sore back. When Ananda concluded his talk and the Buddha had tended to his throbbing back, the Buddha said: "Excellent, Ananda, excellent! You have given an excellent talk to the Sakyas on the disciple in higher training." [75]

Ananda was the archetype of the loyal subordinate who was totally dedicated to his Master. He anticipated the Buddha's every need. Ananda was always there for the Buddha, caring for him, solicitous of the Master's comfort. When the Buddha was suffering from wind on the stomach, Ananda cooked what some accounts describe as rice gruel, while others say it was tekatuka gruel, which contained three kinds of pungent substances.[76] This gruel had helped when the Buddha was afflicted with that ailment in the past.

In this instance, however, Ananda received an infrequent rebuke from the Buddha: "It is not proper for ascetics to prepare meals in the house."[77] The Buddha then issued an order that monks could not cook for themselves. They must remain homeless and rely on the good will of householders for their meals.

Why was it acceptable when Ananda cooked gruel for the Buddha earlier, but not now? It is possible that Ananda could have prepared the previous gruel outdoors, which, technically, was not in a house. Maybe the sangha was traveling in a remote area in which there were no householders. The Buddha seemed to have rules and policies for the sangha covering every possible occurrence; so, he must have anticipated a situation in which no food was available for the sangha. This was a rather puzzling situation.

Ananda's devotion to the Buddha included a famous incident when Ananda was willing to die for the Buddha. Ananda, the Buddha, and Devadatta were cousins. Devadatta was extremely jealous of the Buddha, to a level of psychosis. Devadatta once sent a drunken elephant to trample the Buddha. Ananda threw himself in front of the elephant and the Buddha asked Ananda to move. After the third request, the Buddha "moved him gently from the spot through supernatural powers." Some reports say the Buddha stood in the road and gazed at the elephant as it was charging toward him. The beast suddenly stopped. The Buddha talked quietly to it and gently stroked the elephant's trunk and it walked away without harming anyone. Ananda had also offered his life for the Buddha's in four former lives.[78]

Ananda's primary job was to listen to and memorize the Buddha's discourses and then, when asked, to repeat them to gatherings of monks. Ananda soon learned certain tells of the Buddha that indicated he should ask a question. Ananda knew that an Enlightened One "does not smile without cause," so, one day, as they were walking, Ananda saw the Buddha smile and asked him why. The Buddha responded with a story about a past incident that took place in that area.[79] This is further evidence that Ananda had to be fine-tuned to recognize the Buddha's mannerisms.

The Buddha is said to have made several mysterious distant journeys. On the first leg of one of these journeys, the Buddha and Ananda went up the Ganges River northwest to the town of Hastinapura. From there, they walked further north and west to Rothitaka, and then south to the city of Mathura. While they were staying in Rothitaka, the Buddha left the sleeping Ananda one evening and "taking along his supernatural body-guard henchman, the *yaksa* Vajrapani, he flies off through the air, crosses the Indus River, and visits a whole series of places in what is now Afghanistan and Kashmir" ---all in one night. Furthermore, the Buddha and Vajrapani converted "no fewer than seventy-seven thousand beings."[80] while they were there. The next morning, Ananda was no doubt surprised, perplexed, and perhaps a bit envious when he woke up to learn about the Buddha's exciting excursion the night before.

In an incident that could have been written by Agatha Christie, Ananda solved a jewel robbery. He had been teaching the Dhamma to the wives of King Pasenadi and one day they were not as attentive as usual. Ananda asked them what was wrong, and they told him one of the king's crown jewels had been stolen. Ananda proposed to the king a novel way for the thief to return the jewel. A tent was erected with a large pot of water inside. All the suspects were allowed to enter the tent alone so the thief could drop the jewel into the water. When everyone had entered and left the tent, the jewel was discovered in the pot. Ananda had solved the theft through peaceful means.[81] He demonstrated how to solve a problem nonviolently while also revealing his Inspector Clouseau sleuthing talents.

Ananda was on the path to enlightenment and, although his teacher wrote the book, if there had been any books, Ananda was still a learner. And, like anyone who studies a difficult subject, if Ananda had a breakthrough and thought he understood a complicated Buddhist principle, he could sometimes get cocky. In one incident, Ananda told the Buddha that he thoroughly understood dependent origination, a very complicated Buddhist principle. The Buddha responded with a rare rebuke:

> Not so, Ananda, not so! This dependent origination
> is profound and appears profound; it is truly very
> difficult to penetrate. Because they have not
> understood and penetrated this one principle, beings
> are caught on the wheel of birth and death and cannot
> find the means to freedom. [82]

Ananda once asked the Buddha how far the Buddha's voice would reach in the universe. The Buddha replied that the voice of Enlightened Ones would reach all worlds "with their shining splendor." Overjoyed, Ananda said, "How fortunate I am, that I have such an almighty, powerful Master!" Udayi, one of the Buddha's disciples, immediately criticized Ananda: "What good does it do you, friend Ananda, that your Master is almighty and powerful?" Udayi was pointing out that, instead of praising the Buddha, Ananda should be working on his own enlightenment. The Buddha enthusiastically came to Ananda's defense: "Not so, Udayi, not so, Udayi! Should Ananda die without being fully liberated, because of the purity of his heart, he would be king of the gods seven times or king of the Indian subcontinent seven times. But Udayi, Ananda will experience final liberation in this very life."[83]

This was an extraordinarily emotional utterance by the Buddha, who had extinguished all attachment and desires. He admitted that Ananda was not yet enlightened, but the Buddha predicted that, even if Ananda died before he reached enlightenment, Ananda would enter the God realm. Then, the Buddha made a bold prediction that Ananda would gain enlightenment in this life and, after the Buddha's parinirvanization.

Just the forcefulness of the Buddha's defense of Ananda indicates that the Buddha was extremely sensitive to sangha gossip that Ananda was not enlightened. In fact, Udayi was right. Enlightenment is attained by one's own efforts, not through belief in another person. The Buddha was so upset that he changed his defense of Ananda in mid-sentence. He began by saying that, if Ananda died without reaching enlightenment, he would be a king in the God Realm. He then immediately switched defenses by predicting that Ananda would be enlightened in his own lifetime. This is another example that the Buddha's love for Ananda created some tension in the sangha.

The Buddha once audaciously prophesied that Ananda and Rahula, the Buddha's son, would also become Buddhas someday in the future. An account in the <u>Lotus Sutra</u> describes an occurrence when Ananda and Rahula were part of a large meditation session of over two thousand "voice hearers;" a term used by arhats for unenlightened monks whose knowledge of the dharma ranged from basic (learners) to advanced (adepts). Today, a college classroom filled with a mixed bag of undergraduates, master's students, and Ph.D. candidates might be an accurate comparison. These students had no significant insight into the dharma; so, they could only hear the voice of their teacher and diligently try to increase their knowledge.

During this meeting, in an odd coincidence, Ananda and Rahula thought to themselves at the same time: "how delightful it would be if we should receive a prophecy of enlightenment. [84]Ananda and Rahula rose from their seats, bowed at the Buddha's feet, and said,

> World-Honored One, we too should have a share of this! We have put all our trust in the Thus Come One alone, and we are well known to the heavenly and human beings and asuras of all the world. Ananda constantly attends and guards and upholds the Dharma storehouse, and Rahula is the Buddha's son. If the Buddha should bestow on us a prophecy that we will attain anuttara-samyak-sambodhi, then our wishes will be fulfilled and the longings of the multitude will likewise be satisfied.[85]

In a show of solidarity, the other monks all immediately rose from their seats, moved to a position in front of the Buddha, "pressed their palms together with a single mind and, gazing up in reverence at the World-Honored One, repeated the wish expressed by Ananda and Rahula and then stood to one side."[86]

The Buddha electrified the gathering by predicting Ananda's destiny---perfect enlightenment:

> In a future existence you will become a Buddha with
> the name Mountain Sea Wisdom Unrestricted Power
> King Thus Come One, worthy of offerings, of right
> and universal knowledge, perfect clarity and conduct,
> well gone, understanding the world, unexcelled worthy,
> and trainer of people, teacher of heavenly and human
> beings, Buddha, World-Honored One.[87]

As the Buddha continued a lengthy description of the glorious attributes Ananda would acquire when he became a Buddha, eight thousand bodhisattvas wondered to themselves why the Buddha would announce such a profound prophecy to mere voice-hearers, when he had never said anything like that to the bodhisattvas. The Buddha, of course, could read their minds and explained that he and Ananda went back a long time:

> Good men when Ananda and I were at the place of
> Void King Buddha, we both at the same time conceived
> the determination to attain anuttara-samyak-sambodhi.
> Ananda constantly delighted in wide knowledge [of the
> law],
> I constantly put forth diligent effort. Therefore, I have
> already succeeded in attaining anuttra-samyak-sambodhi,
> while Ananda guards and upholds my law. And he will
> likewise guard the Dharma storehouses of the Buddhas
> of future existences and will teach, convert, and bring
> success to the multitude bodhisattvas. Such was his original
> vow, and therefore he has received this prophecy.[88]

Ananda excitedly thanked the Buddha, in verse:

> The World-Honored One, very rarely met with,
> has caused me to recall the past,
> the law of immeasurable Buddhas,
> as though I had heard it today.
> Now I have no more doubts
> but dwell securely in the Buddha way.
> As an expedient means I act as attendant,
> guarding and upholding the Law of the Buddhas.[89]

Ananda's comment to the assembly that the Buddha caused him to recall the past emphasized his long, intimate relationship with the Buddha. And, just in case anyone in the gathering doubted Ananda's influence with the Buddha, he made it clear that he was the Buddha's attendant only because it was an expedient way for him to guard and uphold the law of the Buddhas as he prepared for his future as a Buddha.

The Buddha's confident prediction that Ananda would be a future Buddha contained basically the same information in the text version and when it was repeated in verse. In Rahula's case, the text predicting that Rahula would become a Buddha began with almost the same wording as Ananda's: "In a future existence you will become a Buddha with the name Stepping on Seven Treasure Flowers Thus Come One..." The Buddha continued with a long list of attributes, like Ananda's, that Rahula would possess when he became Buddha; but the text then veered off, saying Rahula would "offer alms to Buddhas" and would "be the eldest son of those Buddhas," suggesting that it would take longer for Rahula to achieve perfect enlightenment than Ananda. In fact, the Buddha predicted that Rahula would first have to be the eldest son of Ananda before he became a Buddha.[90]

It is obvious that the Buddha backed off from a full-throated endorsement for Rahula. When the Buddha spoke in verse, his less-than-enthusiastic prophecy for Rahula reveals several tantalizing mysteries:

When I was crown prince
Rahula was my eldest son.
Now that I have gained the Buddha way
he receives the Dharma and is my Dharma son.
In existences to come
he will see immeasurable millions of Buddhas.
As eldest son to all of them,
with a single mind he will seek the Buddha way.
The covert actions of Rahula
I alone am capable of knowing.
He manifests himself as my eldest son,
showing himself to living beings.
With immeasurable millions, thousands, ten thousands
of blessings beyond count,
he dwells securely in the Buddha's Law
and thereby seeks the unsurpassed way.[91]

This verse provokes many questions. The Buddha tells the group that Rahula is my eldest son. Since Rahula was his only child, he was, in fact his eldest son; but it seems an odd way to describe the relationship. It leaves the impression that the Buddha had other children, which is not supported by historical records. The Buddha said Rahula would "seek the Buddha way" and "...the unsurpassed way." Clearly, the Buddha did not guarantee, as he did with Ananda, that Rahula would quickly become a Buddha. Does the Buddha's cryptic comment "the covert actions of Rahula I alone am capable of knowing," suggest that Rahula was involved in "covert actions" that could be harmful to the sangha? It is difficult to assign a positive motive to anything described as covert. Is the Buddha subtly questioning Rahula's trustworthiness?

At the conclusion of his discourse, the Buddha said to Ananda and the entire group: "These two thousand voice-hearers who now stand in my presence---on all of them I bestow a prophecy that in a future existence they will become Buddhas."[92] The assembly enthusiastically roared that "our hearts are filled with joy as though we were bathed in sweet dew." [93] In contrast, Ananda must have felt that he had been bathed in ice water. The Buddha's promise to the learners certainly diminished the uniqueness of his earlier prophecy for Ananda.

The ability to sew and repair tattered robes was an important part of a monk's duties. The Buddha once told Ananda to distribute robes to the monks. When Ananda accomplished this task, in the presence of other monks, the Buddha congratulated Ananda for the organized delivery of the robes. The Buddha bragged of Ananda's skill in sewing to a group of monks, proclaiming that Ananda could do several types of seams.[94]

Later, the Buddha saw Ananda positioning the monks in a circle to repair their robes. Concerned that this communal sewing circle could lead to frivolous chatter among the monks, the Buddha swiftly called out Ananda: "A monk does not deserve praise who enjoys socializing, who finds joy in fellowship, finds contentment in it, enjoys togetherness, is pleased with it. That such a monk should attain at will the bliss of renunciation, the bliss of solitude, the bliss of tranquility, the bliss of awakening, in their totality, that is not possible."[95]

The Buddha's reaction might seem harsh, but he was reminding Ananda that step three of the Noble Eightfold Path, right speech, prohibits lies, slander, cursing, gossip, useless babbling, and other empty speech habits. And the eighth step, right concentration, could be achieved only when right speech was mastered, and the mind was quieted to allow concentration. Solitude is the most efficient way to achieve right concentration which leads to stillness of the mind. A simple formula might be right speech + solitude + right concentration = stillness of the mind. Thus, any type of companionship or togetherness or socializing, such as communal sewing, that interferes in one's ability to concentrate is a klesha that must be eliminated. The Buddha could also have been sending Ananda a subtle message that Ananda seemed to take special joy in fellowship with females.

As Ananda's close relationship with the Buddha became apparent in the sangha, he was often used as an intermediary between the Buddha and other monks. In one case, two senior monks at a monastery in Kosambi became embroiled in a disagreement. The pupils took the side of their respective Master and soon the monastery and entire community was feuding. A message from the Buddha telling the monks to stop quarreling was ignored. He traveled to the monastery and when his personal pleas to end the squabble failed, the Buddha retreated alone to the Parileyya forest to spend the rainy season. He met an elephant, who protected him and a monkey, who brought him wild honey for his meals.

Meanwhile, the infighting at the monastery was getting worse. Anathapindaka, a senior monk at the main Jetavana monastery, asked Ananda to entreat the Buddha to come back and settle the escalating tension. Ananda and a large group of monks went to the forest and found the Buddha. He agreed to return to the Jetavana monastery in Savatthi, but he was not in a good mood:

> When one has intelligent companions worth associating
> with, who lead a good life, then one should live with them
> happily and cooperatively. Otherwise, live alone like a
> king who has abandoned his kingdom, or an elephant in
> the forest. There is no companionship with a fool; it
> is better to be alone.[96]

The Buddha's strong defense of associating with intelligent companions might appear to be inconsistent with his earlier criticism of Ananda's sewing circle. But when examined, the Buddha was extolling the virtues of the middle way, i.e., an unemotional clear, relationship with one's peers based on knowledge and respect as opposed to a group of chattering, gossiping monks. The disharmony had made the Kosambi monks very unpopular in the monastery and town, but the Buddha forgave them. And he used the discord as a practical example of the Buddhist doctrine of impermanence: "Some people do not realize that quarrels will fade away by themselves. If you know this, you will cease to have dissension."[97] Everything is impermanent. Disputes will eventually dissipate, so don't become attached to them.

On a different occasion, Ananda summoned a group of monks, who had been reprimanded for being noisy, to meet with the Buddha. When the monks came into the Buddha's presence, they realized that the Buddha was in deep "imperturbable meditation," and they did the same. After four hours, Ananda asked the Buddha to greet the monks. The Buddha and the monks did not respond. Four hours later, Ananda repeated his request. Again, there was silence. At dawn, Ananda prostrated himself before the Buddha and asked that he greet the monks. The Buddha came out of his deep meditation and said: "If, Ananda, you were able to understand our minds, then you would have known that all of us had entered into imperturbable absorption, where words cannot penetrate." [98]

The Buddha's words were a hard slap to Ananda. The Buddha was saying "If you were enlightened, you would understand our minds and would not have interrupted our deep meditation." The Buddha's irritation with Ananda is clear. He had to come out of his deep meditation to answer Ananda's minor request. It is very difficult to understand how Ananda could not be aware that the Buddha was meditating. Anyone who has ever interrupted another's meditation soon learns to be quiet and respectful to the meditator. Common sense and common courtesy should have prevented Ananda from interrupting the Buddha's meditation. This is a prime example of the Buddha's extraordinary patience in dealing with Ananda, who sometimes seemed clueless concerning Buddhist procedures.

The Buddha generally went along with Ananda's suggestions for specific discourses that Ananda thought might help certain monks. But Ananda's requests were not always granted. The details are not clear, but Ananda once asked the Buddha to recite a Sutra for a group of monks. The Buddha refused. Following tradition, Ananda asked two more times. The Buddha refused two more times. He told Ananda that he would not speak the discourse until "an offending monk had been removed."[99]

Asubha is an advanced meditation technique that focuses on the less attractive aspects of things we find attractive. The purpose is to produce balance and dispassion. Asubha is very intense and not for novices. For example, that handsome man or that beautiful woman that gives you lustful thoughts, have snot in their noses, wax in their ears, sweat in their armpits and they had diarrhea or were constipated recently. Not so sexy now, are they? Everyone will become old, ill, and dead.

On one occasion, the Buddha spoke to the monks at Vesali on Asubha. After the discourse, in a weird, tragic event, "a large number of them, feeling shame and loathing for their bodies, committed suicide" Ananda waited until the Buddha had finished his fortnight solitude, before telling him about the suicides. Ananda suggested that it might be useful if the Buddha taught the remaining monks some methods to obtain insight.[100] Ananda might also have suggested that the Buddha calibrate his discourses according to the maturity level of the monks in attendance.

4

Females in the sangha

The Buddha had consistently refused to accept females into the Order and Ananda was enlisted by the Buddha's stepmother to press the case to ordain nuns into the sangha. At this point, we need to digress briefly for some back story to explain the Buddha's motivations and why Ananda would have to be on his A-game when he met with the Buddha to discuss that issue.

India, at the time of the Buddha, had a rigid caste system, in which a person's social standing and ability to earn a living depended upon the caste/class he was born into. There was realistically no opportunity for an intelligent person in a lower caste to move up to a higher caste. Maybe in the next life but forget about upward mobility in this life.

The society was also extremely paternalistic. Women were thought to be inferior to men and were considered untrustworthy and deceitful. Higher-caste wives, mothers, children, and relatives in royal households had their specific roles and were protected and respected. Lower-caste females were forced to take less-than-desirable jobs as servants and dancers, with little respect and protection.

Siddhartha's father, Suddhodana, was a leader of the Sakya clan. The main city in the kingdom was Kapilavatthu, in the state of Kosala, on the northern border of ancient India. Some accounts describe

Suddhodana as a hereditary monarch while others claim he was the elected official of a tribal confederacy. King Suddhodana married his cousin, Maya, who became Siddhartha's mother. She died days after Siddhartha was born and Suddhodana took Maya's younger sister, Prajapati, as his wife. She raised Siddhartha as her own son.

The Buddha was born into and grew up in that culture, so his attitude toward females was a complicated mixture of Indian societal norms and his personal experiences with females as a pampered, handsome, rich, powerful, prince. A huge mental barrier separated his love and respect for his stepmother and the women he encountered daily in his harem. The females in his life were either educated and royal-caste with no real responsibilities or uneducated, lower-caste young women who did what they had to do to survive. Thus, his personal experiences with these two diverse groups of women led to his opinion that, either women were not strong enough to handle the privations and personal dangers inherent in homelessness; or that females would corrupt the sangha with their beauty and sexual intrigues.

When Siddhartha was born, a sage told his father that the boy would grow up to be either a great king or a great religious leader. Not surprisingly, Siddhartha's father preferred great king, so he tried to provide anything his son desired while shielding him from any unpleasantness. From the time Siddhartha was born and into his late twenties, he lived an affluent life in which all his wishes were granted. He enjoyed the pleasures of a harem of young females and plenty of wine.

When Siddhartha was sixteen, in an arranged marriage, his young cousin Yasodhara was chosen to be his wife.[101] "She was a dignified and beautiful young woman, the daughter of a Sakya noble family"[102] For the next thirteen years, Siddhartha struggled with his growing discontent and uneasiness with his privileged life. He felt the dukkha that would later become the first noble truth: Life is suffering. Siddhartha had everything money and power could provide, but he still felt incomplete, out-of-balance. Something was missing.

His father, Suddhodana, made sure that Siddhartha was always surrounded by beauty, calmness, and joy. When Siddhartha travelled outside the palace walls, "care was always taken to clear and decorate the way, and especially to remove anything ugly or unpleasant that might disturb the prince's mood."[103]Siddhartha was in a royal prison; trapped in a gilded cage. His life was not reality. The king's extreme efforts to shield Siddhartha from anything unpleasant led to one of the most famous parables concerning Siddhartha's transformation.

While on an evening chariot ride, or several separate rides, it isn't clear, Channa, Siddhartha's charioteer and confidant, apparently took a route that had not been cleansed of disturbing sights. As a result, Siddhartha saw an old person, a sick person, and a corpse. This raises several unanswered questions: Did Channa deliberately take those unapproved routes to show Siddhartha the reality of life? What is the time frame of the sightings? Did they see all four sights during one ride, or did they see each person on separate rides? Over how many days or weeks or months?

Siddhartha could not forget the suffering of the old person and the diseased person. And the decaying corpse drove home his increasing realization that everything in this world is impermanent. We are all sentenced to a lifetime of infirmity, old age, and, eventually, death. But, on the fourth outing, "he saw a mendicant with upright bearing and a serene and radiant countenance."[104] Siddhartha was astonished. He had never seen anything like it, and he asked Channa to explain this odd figure: "This," said Channa, "is a holy man who has renounced worldly life and entered upon a life of homelessness. Such homeless mendicants devote themselves to spiritual pursuits such as meditation or practicing austerities. They have no possessions but wander from place to place, begging their daily food."[105]

The four sights were burned into Siddhartha's mind. This was the seminal moment in Siddhartha's life when the pieces of the puzzle came together. And it was caused by a random, chance sighting of a homeless monk, who displayed the peace and bliss Siddhartha was searching for. Siddhartha now knew that true happiness could be achieved; but he was still undecided about what he should do. And how to achieve that peace.

The cumulative effects of Siddhartha seeing the old person, the sick person, the corpse, and the monk were slowly coalescing toward a decision that would change Siddhartha Gautama into the Buddha. The event that seemed to seal the deal occurred "one night in the women's quarters, after an evening of entertainment, the prince woke up, and in the still flickering lamp light saw the beautiful women lying about him, asleep in various positions of abandon. One young woman, who still held her lute, lay drooling from one side of her open mouth and snoring loudly. Other women lay propped against the walls or against pieces of furniture. Some had wine stains on their clothing. Others with their rich costumes thrown open lay in ungainly postures with their bodies exposed. In the stupor of sleep, they looked like randomly heaped corpses. The seductive visions of their beauty, which had so long captivated the prince, was shattered."[106]

The true nature of the seemingly sensual, beautiful, women in the harem was revealed as only an illusion. Their painted faces merely masks. Their outward beauty destroyed by their intoxicated unconsciousness. Everything we covet and desire in this reality was starkly exposed as only temporary---a mirage. Siddhartha knew that there was a deeper joy, a deeper happiness; a permanent bliss; but he did not know how to achieve it. Siddhartha then made a decision that would change his life...and the lives of millions of disciples in the future.

In "the full-moon night of the summer month of Ashadha,"[107] at the age of 29, just seven days after his son, Rahula was born [108] "...the bodhisattva, astride Kanthaka and with Chandaka at his heels,"[109] left his wife, newborn son, and privileged life in the palace at Kapalivastu ---"and struck out south through the forest."[110] Siddhartha began the quest that would result in his enlightenment and would lead to the formation of a major world religion.

The preceding passages add some insight into the Buddha's opinions of females. Just like royalty today, the primary purpose of his marriage to Yasodhara was to unite the clans and produce an heir to the throne. He still had a harem of women for fun and games. Women were powerless in that society, valued only for their utility. The women in Siddhartha's harem undoubtedly used their beauty and sensuality at times to control men. Siddhartha saw and probably experienced their manipulation. His personal experiences with these women surely fed his distrust of females.

Years later, the Buddha was under constant pressure to admit women into the sangha. He "warned Ananda that the admission of women would have disastrous consequences."[111] The Buddha feared that females would only create mischief by distracting monks from the search for enlightenment. The memories from his youth of the promiscuous harem women undoubtedly affected his perceptions. He compared females to an "infection on the sangha" and "mildew in a rice field or rust on sugar cane."[112] The Buddha truly believed that if women were admitted, they would eventually destroy the Order.

The Buddha also brought up practical, personnel-oriented concerns. Separate housing would have to be constructed for the nuns (Bhikshunis) at extra cost. In keeping with the Buddha's wary attitude about women, he said Bhikshunis would have to be monitored closely to prevent them from seducing the monks (Bhikshus). The patriarchal attitude of the period prevented the suggestion that sometimes men seduced women. The Buddha honestly felt that "asking men and women to live together in a homeless life while trying to master the natural human passions seemed too much to expect of human nature."[113]

The Buddha was driven, not by misogyny, but by his intense desire to spread the dharma. When the Buddha reached enlightenment, he could have immediately entered nirvana, but he chose to stay in this reality to teach the dharma; to show the world that suffering can cease. To accomplish that goal, he had to disseminate the Dharma to as many people as possible. And to do that, he needed a strong, focused, successful sangha that would continue far into the future. He strongly believed, based on the Indian culture and his life experience, that females would destroy the concentration of the monks and delay their enlightenment.

Despite the Buddha's seemingly fixed position of "no females in the sangha," the social movement to admit women was becoming more intense; and his own stepmother/aunt, Prajapati, was leading the charge. Siddhartha's biological mother, Maya, died when he was born. Maya's sister, Prajapati, was part of the King's harem, so Siddhartha's father took Prajapati as his wife. Prajapati loved and raised Siddhartha as her own child. Prajapati was, in today's terms, a feminist. She fervently supported the inclusion of females into the sangha.

During the fifth year of his ministry,[114] the Buddha returned to his hometown of Kapila, where Prajapati lived. In the five years the Buddha had been traveling and teaching, his father, Suddhodana, had died after becoming an arhat.[115] Alone now, Prajapati invited the Buddha to speak to her and the women of the court. Inspired by his sermon, Prajapati eagerly asked the Buddha's permission to join the sangha, but the Buddha had not yet established an order of nuns.

A few years later, the Buddha returned to Kapilavatthu and ordained five hundred Sakya men as monks, which might have been good for the sangha's growth, but the unintended human result was five hundred wives who now had no husbands for protection and support. The blindsided wives undoubtedly felt the Buddha owed them, since he was responsible for their predicament. Prajapati, along with the Buddha's wife Yasodhara, and the upset five hundred met with the Buddha and strongly requested that he create an order of nuns.[116] The abandoned wives no doubt felt that the Buddha owed them for taking their husbands.

In the custom of the day, Prajapati asked the Buddha three times to allow women to enter the Order. The Buddha refused all three times and, using her family name, gave Prajapati advice that is relevant today: "Do not be eager, Gotami, to obtain the going forth of women from home into homeless in the Dhamma and Discipline proclaimed by the Tathagata."[117] His warning to Prajapati sounds to modern ears like be careful what you wish for.

Prajapati, Yasodhara, and the husbandless wives did not give up. They shaved their heads, put on yellow robes, and, barefoot, followed the Buddha on his journey to Vasalit, almost two hundred miles away.[118] Prajapati then adopted a more indirect strategy.

Prajapati could see that Ananda, who would not become the Buddha's attendant for another fifteen years, had a strong bond with the Buddha. She took a chance and asked this young, newly ordained, unenlightened monk without rank, to press the Buddha to admit women into the sangha. Other accounts indicate that Ananda saw the bedraggled group of women before Prajapati had a chance to speak with him. Their "tear-stained faces, dusty clothes, and swollen feet" [119]"... moved him to take their side."[120]

This incident brings up an important historical insight into the Buddha/Ananda relationship. The trust between the Buddha and Ananda was the culmination of close family ties and encounters between the two in thousands of previous lives. But, even with the long personal history, Ananda still had his work cut out for him. The Buddha was very strong-willed. He almost starved himself to death when he was an ascetic. The Buddha was a brilliant teacher and debater who knew how to effectively reach his audience by asking questions, known today as the Socratic Method, that carefully probe the issue and allow students to arrive at the answer through their own analysis, logic, and disciplined thought. "Buddha often tries to clear the minds of inquirers of false notions and to bring them to see the truth by skillfully directed questions and refutes opponents by entangling them in their own answers."[121]

The Buddha reportedly had extraordinary powers that allowed him to time-travel and to enter the minds of others, so he probably knew why Ananda wanted to meet with him. In preparation for the meeting, the Buddha looked into the past. He discovered that all previous Buddhas had an Order of Nuns. Even more surprising, when he looked back into Prajapati's past lives, he found that, many lifetimes ago, she had aspired to initiate an order of nuns. And, most importantly, her aspiration would be fulfilled during his reign. Consequently, the Buddha might have already decided to allow nuns in the Order and just wanted to hear Ananda and Prajapati justify it.

Ananda also had to consider a very important factor: Prajapati had asked the Buddha three times to admit women into the sangha and he had refused all three times. The Buddha had made his decision. The decisions of a Buddha were, by definition, always correct; so, Ananda was hesitant to pursue the issue. But he had promised Prajapati that he would intervene, and he felt strongly that admitting women into the

Order was the right thing to do. Prajapati and Yasodhara waited outside the door as Ananda entered the Buddha's chamber, still confused about whether and how to approach the topic. Ananda stood nervously before the Buddha. The Master noticed Ananda's discomfort: "What is it Ananda? There is a cloud over your face today.[122]

Ananda summoned his courage and, in a flash, decided to use the Buddha's techniques of argument. He first reminded the Buddha of the love and care Prajapati showered on the young Siddhartha. He knew that if he attempted to play on the Buddha's love for his stepmother with a purely emotional argument, he would fail. The Buddha loved his stepmother, but his enlightenment had removed the fetters of intense desires and attachments. Ananda was just cleverly setting the stage. Although the Buddha's love for his stepmother would not be a deciding factor in his decision, Ananda had still planted the seed.

After introducing the emotional factors, Ananda began to logically build his case:

> Blessed One, my mind keeps
> struggling with a question I cannot
> answer. Is it only men who are capable
> of overcoming suffering?

The Buddha realized that this was not an idle question by Ananda, so he answered directly:

> No, Ananda. Every human being has
> the capacity to overcome suffering.

Ananda continued:

> Is it only men who are capable of renouncing
> selfish attachments for the sake of attaining
> nirvana?

The Buddha knew where Ananda was going, but he played along:

No, Ananda. It is rare, but every human
being has the capacity to renounce worldly
attachments for the sake of attaining nirvana.[123]

Ananda sprung the trap: Then, if both men and women can be enlightened, women should receive equal treatment by being accepted into the Sangha as nuns. "The Buddha must have smiled, for Ananda had caught him with both love and logic."[124]Ananda had seemingly convinced the Buddha for he agreed to admit women to the Order.

Ananda opened the door of the Buddha's room "and there stood the two barefooted women waiting for their reply."[125]This account improbably has the Buddha easily putting aside his many years of opposition to nuns by laughing good-naturedly and telling Ananda: "By all this, you have said and done just as I would have said and done."[126]Other accounts that the Buddha very reluctantly agreed to women in the sangha seem to have more validity as evidenced by the severe restrictions the Buddha placed on the nuns; including making them subservient to even the most junior monk.

Some Buddhist historians argue that it was impossible for Ananda to persuade or convince or manipulate the Buddha to allow females into the sangha. "An Awakened One's mind cannot be changed, because he is always in touch with absolute reality."[127]These scholars contend that what appeared to be the Buddha's resistance or hesitation about admitting females to the Order was just an attempt to emphasize to Prajapati and the women that the holy life contained many dangers and hardships.

Monks often meditated in desolate forests. They had to walk many miles, sometimes on lonely, dusty, back roads, from town to town, to preach the Dhamma. The homeless life of a monk or nun was not a romantic adventure. It could be a serious struggle to just stay alive while simultaneously preaching the Dhamma and striving for enlightenment. Begging for food every day; dealing with the natural elements of rain and blistering heat; possible attacks by wild boars and cobras; and, of course, the ever-present danger faced by travelers then as now: criminals, who viewed unarmed monks and especially nuns as easy prey.

Indian society in this period operated under clear, rigid rules in which everyone was expected to fulfill specific societal obligations and responsibilities. Caste and sex were the determinants. Females served their husbands, produced children, and managed the household. The life of homelessness and seeking enlightenment was not considered a viable option for women. Thus, the Buddha had practical, serious concerns about whether females in the Order would be safe and respected. "To cut loose from their family would immediately expose them to dangers against which they were not considered able to defend themselves; so, if the attitude of their menfolk was possessive, it was also protective."[128] Women of royal birth were especially vulnerable, because they were protected and pampered. Homelessness would be particularly hard on them. The Buddha was trying to get the women psychologically prepared for their lives as nuns.[129]

However, at the end of the day, the Buddha allowed women to join the sangha. He overcame deep-seated cultural prejudices. The Buddha is one of the first world leaders, religious or secular who treated everyone, women, and persons from lower castes, equally. But even though he eventually made the correct moral/ethical decision, the Buddha still grumbled that accepting women into the sangha would shorten the life of the Order from 1000 years to 500 years[130] That, of course, was not the case. Empires with great armies have come and gone; but the Buddhist sangha "is one of the oldest surviving voluntary institutions on earth."[131]

Because of his initial opposition to women in the Order, some present-day authors have accused the Buddha of being a misogynist. It is unwise to impose 21st century social mores to people who lived two thousand five hundred years ago. The Buddha did not hate women. Accounts indicate that he always treated females with respect. He loved his stepmother and wife. The Buddha had specific organizational reasons connected to the longevity of the Order for opposing females in the sangha.

At a time when females had no control over their lives, Ananda was instrumental in giving women a choice of remaining at home or joining the Order of Nuns. All accounts agree that shortly after Ananda was ordained, "he helped the Buddha into allowing the setting of the Order of nuns."[132] He is "remembered especially fondly by the Order of Bhikshunis, and it is said that he often preached to nuns."[133]

Ananda bravely questioned the strong societal prejudices concerning women's rights. He considered women as equals. He courageously lobbied the Buddha with inescapable logic: If anyone can be enlightened, why can't women join the sangha?" There is no moral, ethical defense for not allowing women into the Order. Ananda is hailed, as he should be, as a man ahead of his time; one of the first strong proponents for treating men and women with equal respect. This was an important step forward for females and a major accomplishment for Ananda; but senior arhats considered it a serious infraction of sangha rules that Ananda had to defend at his trial after the Buddha's parinirvanization.

5

Ananda's Temptations

Women found Ananda attractive. His "mildness of countenance"[134] was a factor. A contemporary poem described Ananda as having a "face like a full Autumn moon, Eyes that of a pure lotus flower, the teachings of the Buddha as vast as the ocean, which flows into the heart of Ananda"[135] These attributes often led to extreme frustration for the celibate Ananda and for the equally celibate nuns and potentially non-celibate laywomen who were attracted to him.

Ananda's respectful, gentle mannerisms toward women and his appealing looks made him a powerful recruiter of nuns. Because of his strong desire to help females progress to enlightenment, he asked the Buddha to allow him to teach nuns. The Buddha replied that the teacher must have certain qualifications:

- must be virtuous.
- must have comprehensive knowledge of the Dhamma.
- must be well-acquainted with the Vinaya, especially the rules for nuns.

- must be a good speaker with a pleasant and fluent delivery, faultless in pronunciation and intelligibly conveying the meaning.
- should be able to teach Dhamma to the nuns in an elevating, stimulating, and encouraging way.
- must always be welcome to the nuns and liked by them---that is, they must be able to respect and esteem him not only when he praises them but especially when there is an occasion for reproach.
- must never have committed sexual misconduct with a nun.
- must have been a fully ordained Buddhist monk for at least twenty years.[136]

None of the qualifications required that the teacher be enlightened, so Ananda was assigned the responsibility of teaching nuns. Looking back, Ananda might have regretted the assignment. Ananda's decision to be near females "...brought about some difficulties for him."[137]

Ananda was striving for enlightenment; but the major fetter/ roadblock that slowed his progress appears to be his attraction to females. Sometimes, his gentle demeanor and respectful actions were misinterpreted by women. Ananda seems to have spent much of his time either fighting his sensual urges or fending off advances by nuns and laywomen.

The females usually ended up taking the blame for any "misunderstandings" that arose from their relationship with Ananda. "There were two occasions in which nuns stood up for him without justification against the Venerable Mahakassapa."[138] Since the two occasions are not explained, we must infer that Mahakassapa accused Ananda of sexual misconduct with the nuns. They defended Ananda and apparently accepted responsibility for the incidents. The nuns were forced to leave the Order because "they were no longer able to sustain the necessary impersonal and purely spiritual relationship with their teacher, Ananda."[139] This is just one of many altercations between Ananda and Mahakassapa, who reappears later to oppose Ananda at the First Council.

Difficulty between Ananda and females is graphically described by Sasaki and Goddard in two separate accounts. It is probable that the incident took place after Ananda was appointed teacher of the nuns. I have merged the accounts together in a rough timeline that seems to explain the events.

Ananda had finished his begging rounds and had lunch in Sravasti. He dropped by "a well in the center of the marketplace"[140] for a drink of water before he started the two-mile walk back to camp. At this point, some back-story helps in understanding this event. The Buddha had once rebuked two of his principle disciples, Subhuti and Mahakatyayana, for "showing discrimination toward arhats in their practice of begging."[141] Ananda was very proud of his relationship with the Buddha and "his good name and did not wish to give cause for people having suspicions or for slandering about himself."[142] Ananda was always very careful in his actions to not being shame upon himself and damage his standing with the Buddha.

A young woman named Matangi (Pchiti in some accounts,) "the daughter of a Candali, a woman of the lowest caste,"[143] had drawn her water and was walking away. Ananda stopped her and said "O my sister, I am athirst. Give me a drink."[144]

People of the lower caste were called untouchable for a reason. The fact that Ananda spoke to Matangi and then asked her to draw water for him was a revolutionary act. It violated the established social order for a priest, the highest level of Indian society, to even be near an untouchable; and to accept water from the unclean hands of Matangi was unthinkable.

Matangi, flustered and embarrassed, said she was of low caste and "I fear to offer water---therefore my alms giving carries no virtue with it."[145] Ananda replied, "O my sister, I am a Bhiksu. My mind holds equality with all. To me there is no caste, so I am not seeing a difference but just begging water---Give me to drink!" Matangi gave Ananda a cup of clear water. "Then she washed Ananda's feet and dried them with her hair and rose with an amorous fire in her bosom."[146]

Matangi was in love. She was drawn to Ananda's "youthful and attractive person."[147] She asked her mother, Maudenka, a prostitute[148] and practitioner of the black arts, to cast a spell on Ananda that would cause him to fall in love with her. Matangi's mother was supremely confident in her spell-casting acumen and her witty, sassy reply to her daughter has the comedic structure of a modern situation comedy: "My daughter, there are two kinds of men whom the power of my magical charm cannot move. One is he who has abandoned all his desire; and the other, he who is dead."[149]

But this was a different case altogether and fraught with danger. She tried to explain to Matangi why casting a love spell on Ananda was a really, really, bad idea. First, it was immoral: "I know that Ananda has already abandoned all desire and impurity; and we must reverence those who have abandoned life and death. How then can we have so evil a mind as to bind by a spell such a holy man!"[150]

And, by the way, it could result in the entire Candali clan being executed: "Ananda, the Bhiksu, he whose virtue is so great, is a disciple of a Buddha, and the son of a Raja: and he is revered by Prasenajit, the Raja of Sravasti. If I make Ananda come, spellbound by my charm, and it should become known by the Raja, we, the race of the Candali, will be wiped out."[151] So, based on what seemed to be sound moral and pragmatic reasons, Matangi's mother refused to cast the love spell on Ananda, perhaps hoping that Matangi's infatuation with Ananda would soon pass. It didn't.

Matangi "cried bitterly, "O my mother, if you cannot make Ananda come to me, I have no desire to live." Matangi "ran wildly from the house toward the river" and "plunged forward" into the water to drown herself. Neighbors were pursuing Matangi and immediately rescued her and carried her home, where she "writhed in grief upon the floor." Her mother finally, reluctantly, agreed to cast the spell.[152]

The Goddard account leaves out this preamble, which supplies the motivation for Matangi's infatuation, and begins with the Buddha delivering a discourse to twelve-hundred arhats at the Jetavana meditation hall,[153] presumably the day after Ananda and Matangi met at the well. After deep meditation, King Prasenjit of Sravasti invited the Buddha and his elders, along with wealthy laymen in the city, to a reception and feast at the royal palace.

Ananda, who was usually at the Buddha's side, was not there because he had a "previous engagement in a distant district." When he returned, he found the Meditation Hall empty---no disciples---no food. Ananda set out for the city to beg for food. Simultaneously, Matangi's mother was reciting the spell. Ananda "quietly crossed the dried moat that surrounded the city, entered the city-gate with solemn gravity. He was a noticeable figure in his neat attire and solemn manner as if he was on a special mission to receive some ceremonial offering."[154] This description seems to imply that Ananda, indeed, was in a type of trance; perhaps brought on by the magic spell.

Ananda walked from house to house with his begging bowl. When he reached Matangi's home, he "became fascinated by the charm of the young maiden and entered her house and her room.[155] As she watched from another room, "the heart of Matangi danced with joy." After rouging her lips and adorning her body with jewelry, Matangi quietly entered the room, and the seduction began. To set the mood, she burned sweet incense and scattered lotus petals. She offered Ananda a cushion for his comfort and sat beside him. "It was as though a sheep had been caught by its long fleece. Ananda could not tear himself away from Matangi. Poor Ananda could not move though he struggled."[156]

But, before anything untoward happened, Ananda momentarily came to his senses and "cried within himself," asking the Buddha for help. "With his pure inner vision," The Buddha saw Ananda's plight and sent Manjusri, "one of the oldest of those Bodhisattvas who were following the Buddha, to rescue Ananda." [157]

The Goddard account has the incident ending quickly with Manjusri, the old pro, easily breaking the spell. "As soon as Manjusri reached the house, the magic spell lost its power and Ananda returned to self-control. Manjusri encouraged Ananda and Pchiti [Matangi] and they returned with him to meet the Lord Buddha."[158]

The Sasaki description included much more adventure and drama. The imagery is magnificent:

In the dusk of evening through the gay street of Stavasti, Manjusri marched straight to where Ananda was trapped. The Multitude who had gathered before the house of the Candali, heaping abuse upon Ananda saw, suddenly, the stately figure of Manjusri with his long silvery beard, and his eyes blazing like two suns, and his long staff struck upon the earth. There—stood his holy body, emaciated as the white stork. The mother of Matangi, paralyzed with fear, sank to her knees.[159]

Matangi was sitting beside Ananda and saw her mother's incantation flame die out, and "behind the trailing smoke, she saw Manjusri fixing them with his piercing gaze."[160] But no death gaze from an old monk could stop Matangi. She cried out to Manjusri "I know you come to take my Ananda. Though you be a sage, you cannot take him from me!"[161]

In his soul, Ananda heard "the mantra of the Buddha"[162] and when he opened his eyes, they met with the eyes of the Sage Manjusri. The spell dissolved into the smoke. "As Manjusri held aloft his staff, Ananda stood up. Manjusri turned and walked swiftly from the house and Ananda followed. No one heard the sound of their footsteps."[163]

Although her mother's spell on Ananda was broken, Matangi was still passionately in love with Ananda. "She ran after him through the starlit night, her tender toes stumbling upon the pebbles."[164] Frantically shouting for Ananda, she "came to the place where the Buddha was meditating in the company of the multitude of his disciples. Matangi looked wildly among them for Ananda."[165]

The scene that followed would excite any movie director: "Buddha opened his lotus blue eyes from his deep meditation and looked at the Candali with deep compassion. 'Whom do you seek, my child? You are seeking Ananda. Are you not?'" Matangi replied, "Yes. I am seeking him because I love him."[166]

The Buddha wiped her tears and asked Matangi what she loved about Ananda. "I love Ananda for his eyes and his nose and his mouth and his ears, his voice and his gracious carriage." The Buddha then gently dissected her reply." In his eyes, there are tears. In his nostrils, mucous. In his mouth, saliva. In his ears, wax. In all his body nothing but impurities. If you love Ananda for his body, though you have him as yours, you will have but these impurities. It will profit you nothing."[167]

Matangi listened, understood, and was immediately purified. "All of her desire vanished, and she attained the way of the arahant." The Buddha sent for Ananda. Matangi prostrated herself before the Buddha and said: "because of my ignorance, I pursued Ananda: but I have now been enlightened just as darkness rent by a flame, or as one wrecked at sea reaches the shore."[168]This was an astounding moment. The assembled monks witnessed a woman of the lowest caste cleanse herself of all cankers and achieve enlightenment, simultaneously and instantly.

But the large group of disciples were not pleased. They "cried with one voice, she is a daughter of the Candali who practices the black art. How then has this Matangi attained the enlightenment of an Arahant?" The Buddha informed the group that Matangi "was Ananda's wife through five hundred past incarnations. In all of them, they held one another in honor and loved deeply. Therefore, in this present incarnation, in true enlightenment, they have met again." That explanation satisfied the monks. "All the disciples rose and saluted the Buddha."[169]

This incident shows how the rigid caste rules of that era produced an emotional rollercoaster for men and women. It is likely that Matangi had always been relegated to invisibility because she was born into a low caste. So, when a Brahmin of Ananda's stature asked her for water and treated her with respect, it had a profound effect on her. Maybe she was just a naïve, love-struck, immature, young woman. Or…maybe the simple human kindness Ananda showed to Matangi touched her heart.

This occurrence is also a reminder that socioeconomic level is not necessarily an accurate indicator of a person's moral and ethical conduct. Matangi was from the lowest class, but she immediately achieved enlightenment, because her attachment, a desire to be respected, was extinguished after the Buddha talked with her. This story is a powerful reminder that the Buddha Nature is present in everyone.

The Matangi incident also highlights Ananda's long-time problems with females. And, on a larger scale, it reveals the real personal pressures faced by celibate monks. Ananda was not enlightened, so he had not extinguished the fires of desire. He felt the same urges as other men. Was this desire the fetter that had delayed Ananda's enlightenment? The Matangi incident could have been caused by bewitchment or just old-fashioned man/woman attraction. Considering Ananda's position and responsibilities in the sangha, it was certainly preferable for him to claim black magic made him do it.

The incident with Matangi reappears later. In the <u>Surangama Sutra</u>, edited by Goddard, the Buddha delivers a series of discourses on perception and the mind ostensibly intended to help Ananda in his quest for enlightenment; but the Buddha is addressing a large gathering of monks. This account is a prime example of Ananda's important role as everymonk. The Buddha can gauge the difficulty of his discourses based on Ananda's responses to his questions. The loving nature of the Buddha toward Ananda is clear throughout the one hundred sixty-eight pages of the Sutra.

"When Ananda came into the presence of the Lord Buddha, he bowed down to the ground in great humility, blaming himself that he had not yet fully developed the potentialities of Enlightenment, because from the beginning of his previous lives, he had too much devoted himself to study and learning." He pleaded with the Buddha to "support him in attaining perfect Enlightenment."[170] The Buddha then gave Ananda instruction, while all of the bodhisattvas and arhats, "as numerous as the sands of the river Ganges,"[171] sat quietly and listened.

The Buddha began by saying "Ananda, you and I are from the same ancestral blood, and we have always cherished a fraternal affection for each other. Let me ask you a few questions and you answer me spontaneously and freely. What was it that impressed you in our Buddhist way of life and most influenced you to forsake all worldly pleasures and enabled you to cut asunder your youthful sexual cravings?"[172] Ananda replied

when anyone becomes inflamed by sexual passion,
his mind becomes disturbed and confused, he loses
self-control and becomes reckless and crude. Besides,
in sexual intercourse, the blood becomes inflamed and
impure and adulterated with impure secretions.
Naturally, from such a source there can never originate
an aureole of such transcendently pure and golden brightness
as I have seen emanating from the person of my Lord.
It was because of this that I admired my Lord and it
was this that influenced me to become one of thy true
followers.[173]

The Buddha then began an interrogatory with Ananda concerning seeing and perception. But first, the Buddha said Ananda "must learn to answer questions spontaneously with no recourse to discriminating thinking."[174] This tendency of Ananda to obfuscate rather than answer directly was also noted by Maha-Maugalyayana at Ananda's trial after the Buddha's parinirvanization When the Buddha finished his discourse, Ananda did not understand. "Then the Blessed Lord, in view of the audience, reached out his golden hand and softly stroked Ananda's head, at the same time speaking to him and the great assembly..."[175]

As the Buddha repeated his sermon on the mind, Ananda became overcome with guilt about his earlier dalliance with Matangi. His confession to the Buddha and the congregation held the monks spellbound:

My Noble Lord! I have the honor of being thy
youngest relative and thou hast always treated
me with affectionate kindness. Although I am
now only one of your many converts, thou dost
continue to show thy affection for me. But in
spite of all I have gained mentally, I have not
become liberated from contaminations and
attachments and consequently I could not
overcome the magic spell at the home of a
harlot. My mind became confused and I was at
the point of drowning in its defilement. I can see

now that it was wholly due to my ignorance as to
the right realization of what is true and essential Mind.
I pray thee, Oh my Lord, to have pity and mercy upon
me and show me the right Path to the spiritual graces
of the Samapatti so that I may attain to self-mastery
and become emancipated from the lure of evil myself,
and be able to free all heretics from the bonds of their
false ideas and craft.[176]

The large crowd sat in stunned silence. Ananda "bowed humbly before the Lord Buddha, with hands and forehead touching the ground"[177] The audience "awed into intense excitement, waited with earnest and reverential hearts for the response of the Blessed One."[178]

Suddenly, "there appeared a most marvelous sight that transcended everything that had ever been seen before. The hall was filled with a radiant splendor that emanated from the moon-life face of the Blessed One, like hundreds of thousands of sunbeams scintillating everywhere, and wherever the rays reached immediately there were seen celestial Buddha-lands and all the great Bodhisattvas of all these innumerable Buddha-lands were seen to be each in his own place with hands raised and pressed together expectantly waiting for the words of the Blessed One."[179]

After this extraordinary event, the Buddha explained the principles of rebirth and enlightenment. Ananda was having great difficulty grasping the Buddha's discourse. Ananda's response to the Buddha was honest and direct: "As you can see, I am astonished and confused. And this audience, they are also in doubt. Pray have mercy upon us all and explain yourself clearly for we are only ignorant disciples."[180] The Buddha "laid his hand affectionately upon the head of Ananda…"[181] and once again explained perception and the nature of mind.

Ananda "became very sorrowful and with tears falling, with forehead, hands, and feet touching the ground, he paid homage to the Lord"[182] The holy symbol on the Buddha's chest suddenly shot forth a "glorious, blazing brightness, which radiated forth brilliantly into hundreds and thousands of colored rays"[183] throughout the universe.

The "scintillating splendor"[184]came to rest on the crown of Ananda and each person in the assembly.

Ananda "sat dazed hoping for a clearer interpretation of it in the kind and gentle tones of the Master and he waited with a pure and expectant heart for the Blessed One's further explanation"[185]The Buddha, "in great kindness, let his hand rest kindly on the head of Ananda"[186]and recalled that his first teaching after his enlightenment was to his former traveling companions at the Deer Forest in Sarnath. "The reason why all sentient beings fail to attain enlightenment and Arhatship is because they have been led astray by false conceptions regarding phenomena and objects, which defiled their minds."[187]

After further discussion, Ananda was still confused:

> Now as we listen to the teachings of the Lord
> about Perception of Sight, we become more
> puzzled than ever. We do not understand
> what you mean when you say that our mental
> perception of sight is not our intrinsic Perception
> of Sight. Pray, my Lord, have mercy upon us;
> give us the true eye of Transcendental Intelligence
> and reveal to us more clearly our Intuitive Mind of
> Brightest Purity.[188]

Ananda was so overcome by his inability to understand the Buddha's discourse that he began to sob. He bowed down to the ground and waited for the Buddha's reply. The Master felt pity for Ananda and the younger disciples and recited a Sutra to comfort the monks. Then, in a crucial comment to Ananda, the Buddha summed up Ananda's difficulties in reaching enlightenment:

> Ananda! Though you have an excellent memory,
> it seems to serve only to increase your knowledge.
> You are still a long way from the mysterious
> insight and reflection that accompany the
> attainment of Samapatti.[189]

Ananda memorized the words, but he did not internalize the message. It is analogous to a person who can recall the notes to a song but cannot play the tune or religious leaders who preach love and forgiveness but fail to love and forgive in their daily actions. Later, however, when the Buddha finished his sermon on mind and perception, Ananda and the disciples seemed to get the meaning. They "discarded all their doubts and illusions, realized the true reality of their minds and, because of it, became calm and refreshed as never before. Ananda, as usual, being the natural spokesman, bowed down with great sadness at the feet of the Lord Buddha and addressing him, said:

> Glorious Lord of Great Compassion and Purity.
> Thou hast skillfully unveiled my heart and
> encouraged me by many expedient means even
> as thou hast delivered all who were drowning in
> the depths of the Great Ocean of Suffering...But
> I have failed to enter into this Enlightenment and the
> Lord Tathagata has blamed me for it, saying that it
> was because of my very learning that I have been
> prevented from entering. I am like a man who has
> inherited a magnificent palace through the munificence
> of some heavenly king, but who is unable to take
> possession of it without first passing through the
> door of Enlightenment.[190]

Ananda bowed to the ground and waited, along with the other disciples, for the Buddha's response. The Buddha explained that our bodies are "in bondage" to the elements of earth (hardness), water (fluidity), fire (warmth), and wind (breathing and motion.) These bonds are further divided into the sensations and perceptions of seeing, hearing, tasting, smelling, and touching.[191] We are tied to this physical world by these powerful fetters.

The Buddha went on to discuss how perfect concentration of mind must be used to deal with the destructive influence of sexual lust. The Buddha said "inhibition of sexual thoughts and annihilation of sexual lusts …must be discarded and forgotten."[192] The Buddha then made an extraordinary claim that "when the mind is under perfect control and all indecent thoughts excluded, then there may be a reasonable expectation for the Enlightenment of the Buddhas."[193] Not exactly an iron-clad guarantee; but certainly a strong suggestion that elimination of sexual lust opens the door to enlightenment.

The Buddha also said that if disciples kill sentient beings and eat the flesh, they will not reach enlightenment. "Therefore, Ananda, next to teaching the people of the last kalpa to put away all sexual lust, you must teach them to put an end to all killing and brutal cruelty."[194] Disciples may not slaughter and consume sentient beings (cattle, chickens, or pigs), but they may accept meat from householders on their daily begging rounds if the animals were not killed especially for them.

Toward the end of the Buddha's discourse to Ananda and the monks, he directly addressed Ananda's flirtation with Matangi. Ananda had been under a magic spell that had taken control of his mind. But when senior disciple Manjusri arrived and recited the Lord's Great Crown Dharani, the Buddha said "the bonds that bound you to her were destroyed, her passion for you was ended, and by once listening to my teaching she became enlightened. Although she was a prostitute and apparently had no interest in the Dharma, by the invisible power of my transcendental Dharani, she immediately attained to the perfection of all Dhyana practice"[195]

Ananda bowed down at the feet of the Buddha and said, "My Noble Lord! The reason I have not yet attained perfect Emancipation from arbitrary conceptions of phenomena, since becoming thy disciple, is because of my pride in being known as thy favorite cousin and because of my exceptional learning, so when I was brought under the spell of the old woman's magic, in spite of the conscious purpose of my mind, I was unable to free myself from it"[196] until Manjusri recited the Lord's Great Crown Dharani. Ananda admitted that he still did not know the dharani and asked the Buddha to recite it for the gathering. As they waited, there appeared a most wonderful sight.

From the crown of the Blessed One's head there streamed
forth a glorious splendor in the likeness of a wonderful
lotus blossom, and in the midst of the abundant foliage and
seated in the cup of the blossom was the Lord Tathagata's
Nirmanakaya (appearance body). From the crown of the
Lord's head there radiated outward uncounted beams of
light that shot outward in all the ten directions, and in each
of the bright beams of light were figures of transcendently
mysterious Vajra-gods permeating everywhere in the open
spaces of the universes and suggesting the lightning-like
potencies of all the transcendental powers.[197]

When this vision faded, the Buddha recited the Great Crown
Dharani. He told Ananda and the gathering that "should any sentient
beings in any of the kingdoms of existence, copy down this Dharani
on birch-bark or palm leaves or paper made of papyrus or of white felt,
and keep it safely in some scented wrapping, this man no matter how
faint-hearted or unable to remember the words for reciting it, but who
copies it in his room and keeps it by him, this man in all his life will
remain unharmed by any poison of the Maras."[198]

Early biographers of Ananda note other troubling instances
concerning Ananda and females. An unnamed nun in Kosambi sent
a messenger to Ananda asking him to visit her because she was ill.
When Ananda arrived at her dwelling, he realized that her claim of
illness was false, and she was in love with him and intended to seduce
him. He told the nun that her body had arisen, which meant that her
body was attached to an unhealthy desire, due to four defilements.
The first three, nutrition, craving, and pride could be destroyed by
turning each back on itself, But the fourth cause of body arising, sexual
intercourse, could not put one on the noble path to enlightenment.
The nun understood, "got up from her bed, prostrated before Ananda,
confessed her offense, and asked for forgiveness."[199]

Ananda had to contend with powerful rivals in the sangha. And
his most serious opponents were enlightened arhats. Mahakassapa,
considered "Foremost in Asceticism," had several run-ins with Ananda.

For example, the two monks once visited a nunnery to instruct the nuns. Although speaking in public terrified Kassapa, Ananda somehow convinced him to give a discourse to the nuns. Predictably, Kassapa's presentation crashed and burned. When he finished, a nun complained that he had talked too much and should have let Ananda say something. In a final, stinging insult to Kassapa, the nun said, "it was as if a needle peddler had tried to sell his wares in the presence of the needle maker."[200]

Rather than just ignore the nun's comment, the angry Kassapa warned Ananda to "show restraint" in teaching the nuns or the sangha would initiate an inquiry into his behavior. Kassapa said Ananda "overlooked the danger of personal attachment"[201] in his enthusiastic sermon to the nuns.

This is another case of what really happened. Ananda was considered a good public speaker and must have known Kassapa had problems speaking in public. And the thought of speaking to a group of women undoubtedly increased Kassapa's stress level. But Ananda kept pressing Kassapa to speak and "after initial hesitation,"[202] Kassapa agreed to deliver a discourse to the nuns. Kassapa's sermon to the nuns was disastrous. He was embarrassed by the nuns' reactions and comments. Why did Ananda goad him into it, knowing that Kassapa would probably fail? Did Ananda want to humiliate him in front of the nuns?

Kassapa might also have sensed some physical attraction between Ananda and the nuns. Perhaps he was merely trying to help Ananda recognize the dangers of getting too familiar with females. This is another example that perhaps Ananda's attraction to women had not been extinguished and was contributing to his inability to achieve enlightenment.

Even though Ananda had his own struggles dealing with women, he was still able to help a fellow monk who had fallen victim to sensual desires. Ananda and the Venerable Vangisa went to the king's palace so Ananda could teach the Dhamma to the harem women. Vangisa is described as" having a strong sense of sensuality in his character"[203] and when he saw the beautiful young women, in makeup and perfumed, in their ornate dresses, he had an overwhelming rush of sensual desire.

Since Vangisa was a poet, he spoke with Ananda in verse, using Ananda's clan name, Gotama. He graphically confessed his thoughts of "disrobing and indulging in sensual pleasures:"[204]

> I am burning with sensual lust,
> My mind is all engulfed by fire.
> Please tell me how to extinguish it,
> Out of compassion, O Gotama.

Ananda also had some skills as a poet and replied in verse to Vangisa:

> It is due to an inversion of perception
> That your mind is engulfed by fire.
> Turn away from the sign of beauty,
> The aspect linked to sensual lust.
> See constructions as alien,
> See them as suffering, not as self.
> Extinguish the mighty fire of lust.
> Do not burn up again and again.
> Develop meditation on the foul,
> With mind one-pointed, well concentrated.
> Let your mindfulness dwell upon the body,
> Be engrossed in disenchantment.
> Develop the signless meditation,
> Discard the tendency to conceit.
> Then, by breaking through conceit,
> You will fare with heart at peace.[205]

Ananda said Vangisa's desires arose because he was fixated on the superficial feminine beauty and charms of the harem women, "which manifested as weariness of mind and as a kind of aversion toward the ascetic life."[206] Ananda's prescription for Vangisa was deep contemplation and meditation to probe beneath the fleeting impermanence of outward beauty. This would allow Vangisa to see the "wretchedness and misery lying within"[207] the seemingly attractive surface. Then the fires of desire that filled Vangisa's mind would be extinguished, and he would be better equipped to withstand other worldly temptations.[208] There is no record of whether Ananda's advice helped Vangisa control his sensual desires.

6

The Buddha's Declining Health

At the age of eighty, The Buddha began to have physical problems. His life was winding down. As the Buddha, Ananda, and a large group of monks entered the small village of Nadika, The Buddha was informed that there had been many deaths in the village. The Buddha comforted his lay followers with news about where their deceased relatives were reborn and which ones would reach enlightenment without having to be reborn, and so on.

This procedure quickly began to tire the frail Buddha, so he told Ananda about a teaching known as the Mirror of Dharma, in which "his followers can know for themselves that they will avoid unfortunate rebirths and when and whether they will attain enlightenment."[209]This was not a magical mirror, mirror on the wall. Unwavering faith in the Buddha, the dharma, and the sangha served as a mirror so believers would know how close they were to enlightenment. This story shows the trust the Buddha had in Ananda to remember and repeat this teaching.

Later, the main Sangha was camped near Beluva, a village near Vesali, during the rainy season from July to October. Since there was a famine, the Buddha told the Sangha to spread out to surrounding villages to avoid putting too much strain on the Beluva inhabitants.

The Buddha and Ananda chose to stay in Venugramaka, a village near Vesali. They camped in a mango grove owned by a courtesan named Amrapali, "who was beautiful, graceful, pleasant, gifted with the highest beauty of complexion, well-versed in dancing, singing and lute playing and through whom Vaisali became more and more flourishing.[210] When she heard the Buddha was there, she drove out in a bullock cart to greet him and to invite him for a meal the next day. He accepted. On her way home, she came upon several young Licchavi noblemen who were on their way to ask the Buddha to have lunch with them. Amrapali was driving an unattractive, clunky, work cart and the young, rich guys were "magnificently arrayed in their sumptuous carriages, looking exactly like the gods of Indra's heaven."[211]

This is where the story gets interesting. Amrapali refuses to pull over to the side of the road to give way to the arrogant noblemen. They immediately insult her as mango woman, while demanding that she get out of the way and let them pass. She refuses. A stand-off occurs. In some accounts, she is described as "axle to axle, wheel to wheel, yoke to yoke" with the young men. Other reports claim she is much more aggressive and tries to crash through the carriages, "smashing their banner flags and parasols" while yelling "Let me through. The Blessed One is coming to my house."[212]

The nobles then decide a bribe might work. They offer her a hundred thousand pieces of gold if she will only withdraw her invitation so they can have the honor of serving dinner to the Buddha. A hundred thousand pieces of gold is a lot of money today and must have been an inconceivable fortune in the Buddha's time. But Amrapali refused the bribe, "telling them she would not give up this chance for the whole of Vaisali!" [213]The overbearing young dandies realized that harassing and bribing Amrapali was not effective, so they hurried to the Buddha's encampment, probably assuming the Buddha would cancel his luncheon with the harlot to have lunch with them. But the Buddha declined the young nobles' invitation, saying Amrapali asked him first.

The next day, the Buddha and his entourage went to Amrapali's house and enjoyed a delicious meal, served by Amrapali and her beautiful ladies-in-waiting. Amrapali, who is disrespected by most of the community for her choice of livelihood, was so honored by the Buddha's visit and his respectful conduct toward her, that she gave the Master her stately mansion and mango grove "and became a bhikshuni."[214] The Buddha thanked Amrapali by preaching the Dhamma to her and her ladies-in-waiting.

In some versions of this story, before they visit Amrapali, the Buddha reminds his monks to be attentive and mindful; to prevent being seduced by the alluring females. Other accounts claim the Buddha's lecture was on mindfulness to warn the monks to avoid becoming enthralled by the expensive carriages and ornate clothes of the rich Licchavi nobles, not specifically to beware of Amrapali and her ladies.[215]

This incident reveals that the Buddha was not the hard-core misogynist as he is characterized by some historians. From a purely monetary standpoint, he had more to gain by having lunch with the rich nobles. If they could offer a hundred-thousand-dollar bribe to Amrapali, it is logical to assume that the Buddha could have gotten a big chunk of money from them for the sangha. All he had to do was cancel Amrapali's invitation. And accepting a dinner invitation from a woman of "ill repute" no doubt raised eyebrows in the sangha and the community. But the Buddha kept his word to Amrapali. He was an honorable man, who did not judge others. The chroniclers were very kind to Amrapali. Then, as now, a hefty donation, whether money or a stately mansion and property, usually results in good press coverage.

This event also shows that the Buddha's decisions always centered around what was best for the sangha. His responsibility was to ensure the continuation of the Order. He initially opposed admitting women to the Order because he felt females would interfere with the monks' concentration and would hinder their quest for enlightenment. The Buddha also could have been trying to protect women from the harsh life of a mendicant.

Shortly after the dinner with Amrapali, the Buddha became deathly ill. There are no records indicating a connection between the meal and his illness. He survived with his powerful ability to concentrate[216] As the Buddha was recovering, Ananda, "the most intimate of his disciples,"[217] told the Buddha that he was "confused and afraid" when the Buddha was ill but "I knew you would not leave us without giving us some instructions for the guidance of the Sangha.[218]

The Buddha's response was that of a master teacher: "But Ananda, I have spent forty-five years giving instructions for the guidance of the Sangha. I am not one of those who jealously keep their important teachings in a closed fist. The dharma has been fully revealed."[219] This interaction reveals that the Buddha has given us everything we need for enlightenment. It is also a stark reminder that Ananda is not yet enlightened, or he would have understood. On the other hand, it gave the Buddha the opportunity to explain that enlightenment is available to all. There are no secrets. In this conversation, the Buddha gave a touchingly candid description of his rapidly deteriorating health: "I am old and decrepit like a broken-down old cart that has to be held together with thongs" [220]

As he was recovering, the Buddha had a pivotal conversation with Ananda. He told Ananda that Tathagatas, like himself, could survive to the age of one hundred years, but only if someone asked them to do so. Remarkably, Ananda missed this obvious hint. The Buddha made the same statement again and Ananda again did not ask the Buddha to extend his life. The Buddha hinted a third time and, once again, Ananda failed to understand.[221]

At this point, the dejected Buddha gave up, walked to a nearby tree, and sat down. Mara appeared and always eager to get rid of the Buddha slyly suggested he should just go ahead and enter complete extinction now. The Buddha replied, in so many words, I'll go when I'm ready and I'll be ready in three months. With the deadline set, the world responded with a gigantic earthquake. Ananda asked the Buddha about the quake and the Buddha gave Ananda six reasons for an earthquake. The last reason was that he was going into full extinction in three months.

Ananda finally got it and asked the Buddha to extend his life, but the Buddha replied that it was too late. Ananda asked again and the Buddha replied again that it was too late. Finally, when Ananda asked a third time, the Buddha's patience was gone: "Do you have faith,

Ananda, in the enlightenment of the Tathagata?" Ananda replied "yes." The Buddha's reply was crushing: "Why then, Ananda, do you persist against the Tathagata up to the third time?"[222]

The Buddha still did not let Ananda off the hook. He made it clear who bore the blame for not asking him to extend his life: "The fault is yours, Ananda. Here you have failed, inasmuch as you were unable to grasp the plain suggestion given by the Tathagata and you did not ask him to remain. For if you had done so, Ananda, twice the Tathagata might have declined, but the third time he would have consented."[223] And the Buddha wasn't finished. He listed fifteen other times when he had given the same hint, but Ananda had failed to ask him to remain in the world. [224]The Buddha then gave Ananda a brief lecture on impermanence and concluded: "Further, it is impossible for a Tathagata to go back on his word; in three months' time he shall attain final Nibbana."[225]

This occurrence demands analysis. Why did Ananda, whose job it was to listen closely to the Buddha and remember everything he said, miss those obvious hints on fifteen separate occasions? Was it intentional by Ananda or had the Buddha taught all he needed to teach and decided it was time to go? Perhaps Ananda didn't understand some of the more arcane Buddhist customs since he was not enlightened. Or maybe Ananda's mind just wandered for a minute. Or maybe the Buddhist version of the devil was involved. "In his confusion his mind had been ensnared by Mara, the Evil One, who still had some degree of power over him."[226]Or "Could it be that at just that moment Ananda was so absorbed in the pleasure of being in close companionship with the Buddha that the master's hint failed to register on his mind?"[227]

The relationship of Ananda and the Buddha could be compared to Judas and Jesus. Without Judas, Jesus would not have been arrested and crucified, which would have had a major impact on the Christian movement. Thus, the actions of Judas were essential to propel the narrative. Likewise, the trajectory of the Buddhist movement would have been affected, in some way, if Ananda had asked the Buddha to live another 20 years. Whether they knew it or not, Judas and Ananda were essential players in their dramas. Their actions in the case of

Judas or inaction in the case of Ananda were necessary to accomplish the master plan. At the first council, other arhats did not accept any justification or excuse and blamed Ananda for failing to ask the Buddha to extend his life.

Three months before the Buddha's parinirvanization, Ananda had seven dreams. He asked the Buddha to interpret them: "Buddha, in the first dream, I dreamt that the entire ocean was burning. The flames were so great that they rose all the way to the sky." The Buddha responded, "Ananda, the noble ones do not interpret dreams, but your dreams were indeed strange. The ocean of fire signified that in the future sangha, many are evil, few are good, after receiving offerings, they would fight and argue, just as if this clear and clean water becomes a flame."

Dream #2---"the sun is gone, the world is in darkness, there were no stars in the sky." The Buddha's interpretation was that "the eyes of wisdom will soon fade" because the Buddha and many of his great disciples would enter final nirvana in a few years.

The Buddha interpreted Dream #3 "Monks do not wear robes; they fall into pits and the laymen step on their heads" as "future monks give public speeches but do not follow what they preach. They are jealous of each other, do not respect the law of cause and effect, ultimately, they fell, the laymen rises [sic] and look down on the sangha. They go into monasteries and frame monks and damage the temples." Toward the end of Ananda's life, he encountered a young monk who arrogantly refused Ananda's corrections on a Sutra.

The Buddha said Ananda's fourth dream "the monks robes are incomplete, and they kneel on thorns" meant that "future monks do not wear the holy robes, do not follow precepts, like the worldly pleasures, have wives, this is a big misfortune of the Dharma." Present-day monks may choose to take a wife or remain celibate.

Ananda's fifth dream concerned "...a thick forest, many pigs were digging the roots of the Bodhi tree." The Buddha responded "Ananda, this says that the future monks only cares [sic] about making a living, they sell Buddha statues and Sutras as occupations."

Dream #6---"the big elephants neglects [sic] the small elephants, and the king of the beasts the lion died. Holy flowers fall on the lion's head, but the animals are scared and keep their distance. Soon the corpse develops worms which feed on the lion's meat." The Buddha responded that: "Big elephants neglecting the small elephants, this means in the future Sangha the elders are selfish and would not groom the young. The worms feeding on the lion's meat, this means no other religions can damage Buddhism, but it is our own Buddhists who will destroy my teachings."

The Buddha interpreted Ananda's first six dreams as clear indicators of future turmoil in the sangha. The Buddha might have dreaded hearing Ananda's seventh and final dream---"I dreamt that my head supports Mount Meru, but I do not feel the weight." However, the Buddha was very relieved. "Ananda, this means that Buddha will attain final Nirvana in 3 months' time, all great monks and people will need your help to compile the Sutras."[228] Ananda was a driving force to assemble the Sutras at the first council after the Buddha's parinirvanization

All of Ananda's disturbing dreams came to pass with the Buddha's parinirvanization. Ananda accurately predicted future tumult in the sangha. It appears that Ananda did not pass along the Buddha's explanations of his dreams to the sangha; because, if he had, it is doubtful that the senior monks would have ignored the Buddha's directive and been so adamant that Ananda had to be enlightened to attend the first council.

7

The Buddha's Parinirvanization

efore the Buddha and Ananda started the arduous journey to Kusinara for the Buddha's parinirvanization, the Buddha looked wistfully at Vesali and said to Ananda: "This will be the last time that the Tathagata will behold Vesali. Come, Ananda, let us go to Bhandagama."[229]

As the sangha grew, so did the challenges. As the Buddha aged, the problems intensified. The sangha was experiencing serious personnel issues. The Buddha's top disciples were all growing old. There was a natural jockeying for position and power among the younger members.

The Buddha taught that each person controls his/her destiny, and the dharma holds the answers to enlightenment, not a person. Not the Buddha or anyone else. The Eightfold Path is difficult and requires extreme individual effort. But people then were like people now. They wanted a quick fix. They wanted to listen to the Buddha or speak with him and instantly become enlightened. That was not likely. This discord in the sangha was reaching a dangerous level.

The Buddha and "a large community of monks,"[230]the exact number is not known, had traveled to Pava, and were camping in the mango grove of a blacksmith named Cunda.[231]When he heard they were there, Cunda dropped by to welcome the group. The Buddha "instructed him with talk about the teaching, encouraging, enthusing, and inspiring him." [232]When the Buddha concluded his sermon, a delighted Cunda invited him and the monks for tomorrow's meal. The Buddha's silence indicated his acceptance.

A visit by the Buddha was a great honor for a householder. Since company was coming, we must assume that the host would serve the best food he could afford. That was not what happened. It is assumed that Cunda bought the meat on sale at a local market since the Buddha would not eat the flesh of an animal that had been killed especially for him.

The Buddha's final meal, which directly led to his parinirvanization, is not precisely known. It has been described as "tender boar" or "boar-softness." Some believe it was "either a form of minced pork or a dish of the truffle mushrooms enjoyed by pigs." [233]This introduces the possibility that the Buddha consumed poisonous mushrooms. One account states that the Buddha was "served a rich meal that included mushrooms. It was after, and perhaps because of, this meal that the Buddha's illness returned." [234]

Curiously, as the Buddha and his monks were being seated, the Buddha said: "Cunda, serve me with the tender boar you have had prepared, serve the community of monks with the other sorts of food you have had prepared;" [235] described as "sweet rice and cakes" in one account. [236]

The Buddha then made an extraordinary and mysterious request of Cunda: "Whatever tender boar you have left, bury it in a hole. I do not see anyone in this world with its gods, its Mara and Brahma, anyone of this generation with its ascetics and Brahmans, its princes and peoples who could properly digest it once eaten, except the Tathagata." [237]Then, after telling Cunda and everyone within earshot that, basically, his meal was spoiled, the Buddha dutifully consumed the rotten food, whatever it was, served by Cunda. Literally, it was the Buddha's last meal.

The Buddha was still very weak from his earlier illness. Did the Buddha truly believe his powers as a Tathagata would protect him from food poisoning, as he told Cunda? Some historians believe the Buddha engineered his last meal because he was ready to enter parinirvanization.[238]

Food poisoning was rampant and often fatal in that time. Twenty-five hundred years ago, there was no understanding of proper food handling. There was no refrigeration of meats. There was no way to effectively treat illnesses. The Buddha had a history of gastro-intestinal complications and dysentery. It is the actions of everyone involved in the Buddha's poisoning that raises questions.

Did Cunda accidentally serve poisonous mushrooms that grew near the boar droppings?[239] In ancient India, just as now, one must be very careful to identify good mushrooms from bad ones. But it strains credulity to propose that Cunda could not tell the difference between edible and poisonous mushrooms. The consensus is that the fatal meal was likely pork meat that had turned rancid. Whatever the entrée' was, it was definitely not a life-prolonging elixir or rice pudding. Within a few hours the Buddha suffered a violent attack of gastric illness with dire pain and severe bleeding of the bowel. He bore the pain with equanimity, mindful and aware."[240] He parinirvanized shortly thereafter.

This incident brings up a lot of uncomfortable questions. The Buddha had a policy that, when his monks were on their begging rounds, they were to accept any food householders gave them. Devadatta, the Buddha's nemesis, who constantly questioned the Buddha's directives, had once recommended a requirement for the sangha that monks must be vegetarian. The Buddha rejected it, logically reasoning that, at a time when people could literally starve to death and monks had to beg for their food, to demand a certain type of food, to ask for a menu, in effect, would be very insulting to the householder. Beggars can't be choosers. To this day, a vegetarian diet is not required for Buddhists.

However, it would seem practical to at least make sure the offered meal was not spoiled. Was the Buddha was so locked into the moral and ethical tradition of accepting any food, that he ate the spoiled meal because he did not want to embarrass Cunda? The Buddha did not want Cunda to feel guilty or for others to blame him for the Buddha's death. Even as the Buddha was quickly parinirvanizing, he told Ananda to reassure Cunda that the person who served the Buddha's last meal earned only good karma.

Spoiled meat is easy to spot by just looking at it or smelling it. If Cunda somehow overlooked the stench of the meat before serving it, he certainly knew it was bad when the Buddha told him not to serve it to anyone else and to bury it. Why didn't Cunda offer the Buddha some of the other, unspoiled food?

The serving of obviously spoiled food to the Buddha brings up a disturbing conspiracy theory. Some modern scholars believe the Buddha was assassinated. "They see the loneliness of the Buddha's end and the remoteness of the location as a sign of a distance between the Buddha and the sangha."[241] and believe that "he died a violent death," as did Moggalana. In fact, Srigupta, a member of a heretical sect, who was jealous of the Buddha's success, earlier tried and failed to "take the life of the Master by poisoning his food and misleading him into a pit of fire."[242] The poisoning aspect of this early assassination attempt is an eerie precursor to the Buddha's fate.

If the Buddha was assassinated, the prime suspect is easy to identify: Devadatta. This was a tumultuous period in the early sangha. The Buddha's declining health and advanced age invited rebellion. There was an old-fashioned power struggle going on in the sangha. Devadatta was leading the insurrection. Devadatta had twice tried and failed to murder the Buddha. Thus, a disturbing, but plausible, theory emerges in which Devadatta hired Cunda to poison the Buddha. Devadatta was trying to wrest control of the sangha from the Buddha; even suggesting that the Buddha retire on the grounds of old age. The Buddha's response left nothing to the imagination: "I would not even ask Sariputta and Moggalana to head this community, let alone a lickspittle like you"[243] In a different, more colorful account of that incident, the Buddha, ever the wordsmith, responded that, if he would not even turn over the sangha to one of his trusted disciples, why would he give it to a "vile drooler of snot" such as Devadatta?[244]

Foiled in his attempt at an internal takeover, Devadatta then tried to destroy the sangha by leaving with many monks. Sariputra and Moggalana, two of the Buddha's oldest and most trusted disciples, quickly brokered a deal with the monks to return to the sangha. Then, in a crushing blow to the ill and fragile Buddha, shortly before his paranirvanization, Moggalana was murdered in a rockslide, which bore Devadatta's fingerprints since he had earlier tried to kill the Buddha by dumping rocks on him. Then Sariputra died and the Buddha joined him within two weeks. It is not a stretch of logic to propose that Devadatta hired Cunda to murder the Buddha. The suggestion that Cunda did not realize the meat was bad does not pass the smell test. The only logical conclusion is that Cunda served spoiled meat to the Buddha knowing that the Buddha would feel obligated to consume it.

The deaths of Sariputra and Moggallana was a devastating blow to the Buddha. "None of the inner circle was left except for Ananda. The texts try to disguise it, but there were no more excited crowds and colorful dinners with friends. Instead, the Buddha and Ananda, two old men, struggled on alone, experiencing the weariness of survival and the passing away of companions which constitutes the true tragedy of old age."[245] The Buddha was simply tired. He was, after all, eighty years old. The traveling, mostly by foot, was exhausting. He was entering the final phase of his life.

The most troubling aspect of this episode is: Why didn't Ananda speak up? Ananda was probably sitting beside or very near the Buddha. Ananda must have seen and smelled the rotten meat. Ananda's job duties specified that he would not consume any of the Buddha's food, but that was to reassure the sangha that Ananda did not accept the position of the Buddha's attendant only to get extra and/or better food.

The Buddha never tried to force his views on anyone. He taught that we must reach enlightenment through our own study, thought, meditation, and efforts. No one can do it for us. The Buddha obviously knew the meat was bad, but he expected Ananda to recognize that fact too. As always, the Buddha let his disciples reach their own decisions. He was waiting for Ananda to step up.

This, however, was a totally different situation. Ananda would have buried the spoiled food, not eat it. Ananda's job was to protect and care for the Buddha. When the Buddha allowed Ananda to be his attendant, the Buddha praised Ananda to Maha-maudgalyayana: "He will offer only that food to the Buddha which will be best for him. He will know whether certain foods will hinder the Buddha's eloquence in speech or give him more vigor."[246]

If Ananda had taste-tested the Buddha's food or even just smell-tested it, he could have gently suggested that the Buddha accept the servings intended for the monks. Ananda could have saved the Buddha's life; but he sat there and watched, while the infirm, aged Buddha ate spoiled food. The outcome could easily be predicted.

Since the Buddha was highly enlightened, karma, either positive or negative, had no effect on him. But he was still subject to the karma of others resulting from the dependent arising of actions. The Buddha had powerful mental powers allowing him to view all the previous interconnected actions that led to this specific moment-in-time to this specific meal.

The Buddha could also see the future. He knew what was going to happen and he could control his responses to affect the outcome. He could choose to not consume the food, or he could have considered the chain-of-events that occurred before and would occur after he ate the food, to be his destiny. Perhaps Ananda's failure to intervene was just a link in the succession of dependent events. Perhaps it was all meant to be.

Scholars critical of the murder conspiracy theory note that just because the Buddha became indisposed after eating the meal prepared by Cunda, it doesn't necessarily mean that the meal was the cause. The Buddha was still weak and recovering from a bout of serious dysentery prior to his dinner with Cunda. Perhaps this was just a tragic coincidence. Critics of the murder theory also say the Buddha told Cunda to bury the remainder of his meal because the gods had added a special elixir to "fortify the Buddha," which made the meal indigestible to ordinary humans and, even the gods. The Buddha also made a point of telling Ananda to reassure Cunda that he was not responsible for the Buddha's parinirvanization.[247]

After the inedible dinner served by Cunda, the Buddha seemed anxious to get out of Rava as soon as possible: "Come, Ananda, we shall move on to Kusinara"[248]The Buddha was accompanied by his usual retinue of monks, "but apart from Ananda, no senior member of the Order was with him."[249]

Perhaps due to his lack of enlightenment, Ananda's behavior seemed strange, and he asked the Buddha irrelevant, inappropriate questions during the Buddha's pre-parinirvanization period. For example, on the way to Kusinara, the Buddha "fell seriously ill, passing blood in his stools, and suffering severe pains as though he were close to death."[250] They stopped to rest, and the Buddha asked Ananda to get him some water from a nearby stream. Instead of quickly and quietly getting the water, Ananda had a better idea. He replied that five-hundred carts had just passed through the nearby stream and the water was stirred up and muddy. Instead, Ananda suggested they make a short trip to the River Katuttha, right down the road, where the water was "clean and with easy banks, it is delightful, and its water is clear, good, and cool. There the Blessed One can drink water and cool his limbs."[251]

Well, that's not what the Buddha asked for and it's not what he wanted. He was thirsty now, so he asked Ananda a second time for a drink of water. Ananda's reply was the same. The very ill and parinirvanizing and thirsty Buddha asked a third time and Ananda finally agreed. This incident did not reflect positively on Ananda. His job was to serve the Buddha, not to second-guess him.

Although the nearby stream had been flowing slowly and the five-hundred carts had churned the water into mud when Ananda had checked it earlier, when he approached it now, the stream flowed quickly and was "clear, bright, and free of mud"[252] Astonished, Ananda took the bowl of clean, cool water to the Buddha and praised the Blessed One's power.

Meanwhile, a young man named Pukkusa, a lay follower of the Buddha, saw him drinking his well-earned water, and stopped to chat. Pukkusa presented the Buddha with "two robes of cloth of gold, burnished and ready for wear"[253] In the Caras account, the Buddha instructed Pukkusa to clothe him in one garment and Ananda in the other. A different version has Ananda accepting the robes. When the young man left, Ananda offered both cloaks to the Buddha, in keeping with his original employment agreement that Ananda should not be given any robes that had originally been offered to the Buddha.[254]

Both accounts marvel at the Buddha's glowing body. "And the Tathagata's body appeared shining like a flame, and he was beautiful above all expression."[255]Ananda remarked that the bright, lustrous golden robes seemed to fade in color when they touched the Buddha's body.

"How wonderful a thing it is, Lord, and how marvelous, that the color of the skin of the Blessed One should be so clear, so exceedingly bright! When I placed this robe of burnished cloth of gold on the body of the Blessed One, it seemed as if it had lost its splendor!"[256]

The Buddha responded: "There are two occasions on which a Tathagata's appearance becomes clear and exceeding bright. In the night, Ananda, in which a Tathagata attains to the supreme and perfect insight, and in the night in which he passes finally away in that utter passing away which leaves nothing whatever of his earthly existence to remain."[257]

An astounding event had just occurred. Only one person in the entire world, Ananda, knew that the Buddha would parinirvanize that night. Ananda's reaction to this staggering news flash is not recorded. Did Ananda once again fail to understand the meaning of the Buddha's words, as he did earlier when the Buddha hinted that he could live longer if someone just asked him, and Ananda did not get the hint and did not respond in time?

Since Ananda was not adept at reading subtle hints, the Buddha told Ananda, in detail, what was going to happen. "So, tonight, in the last watch, at Upavattana, the sal grove of the Mallas at Kusinara, between two sal trees, the final nibbana of the Tathagata will happen"[258]Once again, Ananda's reaction is not recorded.

The Buddha and Ananda continued their journey to Kusinara. The Buddha, increasingly weak and quickly fading, took his last bath in Hiranyavati River and lay down on his right side to rest. Even as he was becoming parinirvanized, the Buddha was concerned about others. He instructed Ananda to visit Cunda, the blacksmith, and reassure him that the person who served the final meal to the

Buddha before he entered nirvana "is something that counts for you, something very advantageous to you. I have heard directly from the Blessed One."[259]After the Buddha rested, they continued their trek to Kusinara.

The Buddha's violent dysentery forced them to stop near a grove of sala trees[260]just outside Kusinara. The Buddha told Ananda to prepare a bed for him "between two sal trees with the head to the north. I am tired and must lie down."[261]Ananda did so and the Buddha "reclined on the ground between two trees"[262]"on his right side...and his two feet carefully placed on top of each other."[263] "These trees were in full bloom, though it was not the season for their flowering; heavenly strains and odors filled the air, and spirits unseen crowded round the bed."[264]

The reality and the finality of the Buddha's impending parinirvanization finally settled in. Ananda leaned against the Buddha's death bed and wailed:

> Too soon...too soon the Blessed One will attain *parinirvana!* Too soon the Eye of the World will be put out! In the past, monks from various regions used to come from all over to see and to venerate the Blessed One, and the Blessed One would preach the Dharma to them...But from now on those who used to come to listen to the Buddha will have heard that he has attained parinirvana, and they will no longer make the journey. Thus, the great rejoicing in the Dharma will cease.[265]

Ananda did not grasp the obvious. The reason he had spent most of his life memorizing and repeating the Buddha's discourses, was to ensure that the Buddha's words would continue after the Buddha was gone. It was not necessary for the Buddha to be alive for anyone to reach enlightenment. Each person had the ability and individual responsibility to seek nirvana. The Buddha just provided the roadmap through his Sutras, the Four Noble Truths, and the Noble Eightfold Path.

Buddha, once again, eloquently comforted Ananda:
But, Ananda, you must know that I will never leave
you. How can I go anywhere? This body is not me.
Unlimited by the body, unlimited by the mind, a
Buddha is limitless and measureless, like the vast
ocean or canopy of sky. I live in the dharma I have
given you, Ananda, which is closer to you than your
own heart, and the dharma will never die.[266]

The Buddha was at the end of his life. Although his
parinirvanization had begun, the Buddha still answered numerous
questions from the assembled monks. Ananda noted that monks
could currently travel to wherever the Buddha was staying during
the rainy season to speak with him and ask questions. Where would
they go after the Buddha's parinirvanization? The Buddha replied
that there are 'four places that should be seen by a faithful man of
family that will stir his heart. Those four places are: the Tathagata's
birthplace [Lumbini]; the place where the Tathagata was enlightened
[Buddhagaya]; the place where the Tathagata turned the wheel of
truth [Sarnath]; and the place where the Tathagata attained nirvana
[Kushinara]"[267] Those sites served a more important function than just
an emotional pilgrimage for believers. The Buddha emphasized that
"all those who die with faithful hearts while they are on pilgrimage
to a shrine will at the breaking up of the body after death be born in
a happy realm, a heaven world."[268]

The fading Buddha showed he was still in charge when he
reprimanded a senior monk. The elder Upavana, who, according to
some accounts, had been the Buddha's attendant before Ananda, was
standing in front of the Buddha, fanning him. The Buddha snapped,
"Move away, monk. Do not stand in front of me." Ananda, shocked
by the Buddha's remarks, asked why he had rebuked Upavana. The
Buddha replied that:

right now, myriads of deities are looking down from the
sky, and, upset, they are grumbling: The appearance of
fully enlightened Buddhas in the world is as rare an event

as the blossoming of the udumbara tree, and today, this buddha is going to enter parinirvana in the middle watch of the night. But this prominent monk is standing in front of him, so that we…are unable to see the Blessed One or to approach and pay homage to him. That is why I asked the Venerable Upavana to move.[269]

Here, we must remember that, although the deities, devas and asuras, are in the two highest and most pleasant realms for those who died unenlightened, they had to depend upon their human senses, rather than having the power to mentally tune in to the Buddha's parinirvanization. They all had to jockey for the best viewing position in front of the giant celestial wide-screen TV.

The Buddha's high regard for Ananda is revealed in an interaction between the two men as the Buddha's parinirvanization got closer. The Buddha asked, "Where is my Ananda now?" In one account, Ananda is leaning on a pillar, weeping, outside the Buddha's room.[270]Another version has Ananda, with a fan of "long white hairs," weeping, sitting beside the Buddha.

Ananda was frightened by the Buddha's imminent nirvana because the Bhiksus could no longer seek counsel from the Buddha. Ananda also feared the loss of his protector: Ananda pours out his heart in the darkness. "Here I am a trainee with work still to do, but my teacher, the one who shows me sympathy, is about to attain final nibbana."[271]For most of his adult life, Ananda had served the Buddha. The future without the Buddha terrified Ananda. "How will it be with me when it is not possible for me to serve him?"

A monk brought Ananda to the Buddha, where Ananda delivered a heartfelt tribute to his Master:

> Deep darkness reigned for want of wisdom, the world of sentient creatures was groping for want of light; then the Tathagata lit the lamp of wisdom, and now it will be extinguished again, before he has brought it out.[272]

As always, the Buddha comforted Ananda:

> O Ananda, you must not weep, and you must not be anxious and troubled; for, Ananda, you have served me faithfully in both word and deed; and have devoted yourself to me with a single mind so that many times, I have felt infinite relaxation. If, back in the most remote period of time, there has been a personal attendant to any Buddha who had no attachment and had highest enlightenment, that attendant could not have been better than my Ananda; and if in the great future, there shall be a Buddha who has no attachment and who has highest enlightenment, he can have no personal attendant like you, my Ananda. I am at present the Tathagata who has no self-attachment and has highest enlightenment, and he can have no better self-attendant than you, yourself.[273]

This passage shows the Buddha's deep affection for Ananda, but it also clearly points out that Ananda was not enlightened. Ananda wept at the Buddha's impending nirvana. In everyday language, Ananda thought the Buddha was dying. If Ananda had been enlightened, he would have realized that the Buddha was entering another dimension: nirvana, a glorious paradise devoid of samsara and suffering.

Another clue that Ananda is not enlightened is his extreme concern about himself. He had not extinguished the duality fetters revolving around the self. He believed that devotion to a person-the Buddha-was required to achieve enlightenment. But that belief was incorrect, and the Buddha had already left clear instructions about how to achieve nirvana: The Four Noble Truths and the Noble Eightfold Path. If Ananda was enlightened, he would have understood.

After the Buddha comforted Ananda, he addressed the assembly of monks and gave Ananda what can only be described as a strong personal recommendation:

> Those Blessed Ones who were perfectly awakened
> arahats in the past also had their special attendants,
> just as I have Ananda. Those Blessed Ones who will be
> perfectly awakened arahats in the future will also have
> their special attendants, just as I have Ananda. Monks,
> Ananda is skilled, he knows when is the right time for
> monks to come and see the Tathagata, when is the right
> time for nuns...for laymen...for laywomen...for a king,
> for royal ministers, for religious leaders, for their disciples.[274]

Oddly, Ananda responded to the Buddha's effusive praise by once again second-guessing the Buddha's choice of the town where he would achieve parinirvanization. As Ananda did earlier at the stream, he said there were much better choices: "Sir, the Blessed One should not attain final nibbana in this mud-wall town."[275] The Buddha said, "Ananda, do not say that this is a mud-wall town, a remote, provincial town." The Buddha went on to explain to Ananda the merits of Kusinara. This was another example of Ananda's attachments to emotions and desires that continued to delay his enlightenment.

The Buddha told Ananda to "go into Kusinara and tell the Mallas there that tonight, in the last watch the final nibbana of the Tathagata will happen. Tell them that they must come and not later regret that, although the Tathagata attained final nibbana in the vicinity of their village, they didn't get to see him in his last hours."[276]

The Mallas reacted to Ananda's news of the Buddha's impending parinirvanization with uncontrolled grief. "The Mallas, and their sons and daughters and their wives felt wretched and unhappy and were overcome with sadness. With disheveled hair some spread their arms wide and called out; they fell to the ground, broken, and rolled back and forth."[277] Not surprisingly, all of them wanted to see the Buddha before he parinirvanized.

In an example of his organizational abilities, Ananda decided that "I had better divide them into various family groups and then present them to the Blessed One to pay their respects, announcing that a Malla of such and such a name along with his sons, his wives, his retinue, and his friends bows down at the feet of the Blessed One."[278]Even though Ananda tried to lessen the strain, this meet and greet was very tiring for the Buddha, whose parinirvanization was increasing.

Ananda was a zealous protector of the Buddha. Sometimes, however, he appeared to overstep his authority. Since he was not enlightened, he did not have the supernatural ability of mental discernment to evaluate, from a spiritual standpoint, who should see the Buddha. Ananda used only one criterion to decide who would be allowed to visit the Buddha: "Is the Buddha too tired?" He could not sense whether a visitor could be helped along the path to enlightenment by talking with the Buddha. This left Ananda in a very precarious position. Each had a job to do. Ananda wanted to protect the Buddha's health, while the strong-willed Buddha understood his mission was to lead seekers to *nirvana*.

This conundrum is well-illustrated by an incident that occurred when the Buddha was preparing for his parinirvanization. A wandering old ascetic named Subhadda, who was not a follower of the Buddha, approached Ananda. The accounts indicate that Subhadda was an irascible, cranky old fellow. Subhadda asked Ananda if he could meet with the Buddha because "a particular doubt has arisen in me, but I feel confident the ascetic Gotama can teach me the Truth in a way that will allow me to get rid of this doubt. Good Ananda, I should like to be permitted to see the ascetic Gotama."[279]Ananda refused: "Enough, Subhadda. Do not bother the Tathagata. The Blessed One is tired." In the tradition of the day, Subhadda asked a second time and a third time. Ananda's answer was always the same: "No!"

The Buddha overheard this exchange: "Enough, Ananda. Do not refuse Subhadda. He should be allowed to see the Tathagata. Everything Subhadda will ask me, he will ask only out of concern to understand, not to bother me. And once I am asked, whatever I shall explain to him he shall quickly understand." One can imagine that Ananda was not particularly happy about being overruled by the Buddha. We can also speculate that Ananda's tone of voice might not have been upbeat when he went to Subhadda and said, "Go Subhadda. The Blessed One gives you his permission."[280]

Subhadda asked his questions and the Buddha answered most of them. For some of the more esoteric inquiries, the Buddha gave his stock answer of "Don't worry about that. It isn't important to seeking enlightenment." Subhadda understood and the Buddha explained the dharma to him. Subhadda immediately converted to Buddhism. Ananda bestowed the going forth ordination on Subhadda, who might have tried to soothe Ananda's ruffled feelings of being overruled by the Buddha with praise for Ananda: "It is something that counts for you, Ananda, something very advantageous to you that you have been anointed as pupils in the presence of the Teacher." Subhadda quickly accomplished the higher ordinations and soon became an arahat. "He was the last of the direct disciples of the Blessed One."[281] Ironically, after the Buddha's parinirvanization, Subhadda repaid the Buddha's kindness with cruelty, as will be explained later.

As the Buddha continued to clear up institutional details before his parinirvanization, a curious exchange occurred between the Buddha and Ananda. Rather than ask the Master about important theological and philosophical issues, Ananda was concerned first about how the Buddha's body should be handled. The Buddha told Ananda to stay focused:

> Ananda don't concern yourself with the Tathagata's funeral. There are knowledgeable rulers, knowledgeable brahmans, and knowledgeable householders too who are committed to the Tathagata---they will conduct the Tathagata's funeral.[282]

Even in his last moments of life, the Buddha urged Ananda to concentrate on his enlightenment: "You should strive for the true goal, you should be devoted to the true goal. You should live applying yourself to the true goal, determined, attentive."[283]

Then Ananda broached a subject that appeared to always be on his mind: How should monks interact with females:

> "Sir, how shall we conduct ourselves with regard to women?"
> "By not looking, Ananda."
> 'But when we look, sir, how shall we conduct ourselves?"

"By not talking, Ananda."

"But when we talk, sir, how shall we conduct ourselves?"

"Mindfulness must be established, Ananda."[284]

To the end of his life, the Buddha maintained his wariness of women. And Ananda was still apparently bedeviled by impure thoughts about females. Whether these conversations indicate a serious attachment for both men is open to speculation.

Ananda was worried about who would teach the Dhamma when the Buddha was gone. The Buddha tried to reassure the sangha that, although he was preparing to be extinguished, his teachings would live on: "...the Dhamma and Vinaya will be your teacher after I am gone."

In another version of the same discourse, the Buddha addresses who will lead the sangha when he is parinirvanized: "It may be that after I am gone some of you will think: Our Master has attained parinirvana; we are now without a teacher, without hope of salvation! You should not see things in this way. The list of precepts to be recited every fortnight, which I taught you, will henceforth be your Master and your salvation."[285]

During this interchange, the Buddha revealed that, although the Dhamma and Vinaya were sufficient to achieve enlightenment, in the future, another Buddha will appear to teach all sentient beings:

I am not the first Buddha who came upon earth, nor shall I be the last. In due time, another Buddha will arise in the world, a Holy One, a supremely enlightened One, endowed with wisdom in conduct, auspicious, knowing the universe, an incomparable leader of men, a master of angels and mortals. He will reveal to you the same eternal truths which I have taught you. He will preach his religion, glorious in its origin, glorious at the climax, and glorious at the goal, in the spirit and in the letter. He will proclaim a religious life, wholly perfect and pure; such as I now proclaim.[286]

When Ananda asked how the future Buddha can be recognized, the Blessed One said: "He will be known as Metteyya, which means 'he whose name is kindness'"[287]

The Buddha's final days were filled with visitors coming to pay homage to him. He did not appoint an official successor; perhaps out of concern that the sangha would become a cult of personality. The Buddha had consistently stressed to the monks that enlightenment was achieved by following the Noble Eightfold Path, not through belief in an individual. He did, however, institute new policies to ensure the smooth operation of the sangha. In the past, greetings and conversations between junior and senior monks could be informal at times. The Buddha felt seniority should now determine how monks addressed each other: "The senior monks could address the junior ones as "friend" or by their names, while the junior ones should use "venerable sir."[288]

This might have been an effort by the Buddha to ensure the continuance of the Order by creating a hierarchy based on merit and achievement; rather than "the personal qualities that monks or nuns may have."[289] This was the Buddha's message to the sangha and Ananda, that, when he was gone, the Order must use what would be described today as a military chain-of-command. Thus, rank (enlightenment) and time-in-rank (seniority) determined one's rise in the sangha; not who a person knew.

In his final moments of physical existence, the Buddha still maintained his control over the sangha. He told Ananda that monk Channa, the Buddha's charioteer before his enlightenment, must be punished for breaking a rule: "When I am gone, the highest penalty should be imposed on Channa. Let him say what he likes, but the brethren should not speak to him or exhort him or admonish him."[290] This was an early version of excommunication or, in a present-day term, ghosting.

With Ananda by his side, as the Buddha was slowly entering final nirvana, he encouraged the monks to ask him any question. "Do not later regret that, although your teacher was right in front of you, you were not able to put your questions to the Blessed One.[291] The monks were silent. The Buddha repeated this incredible offer a second and third time. The monks remained silent.

In case the sangha might be reluctant to ask the Buddha what might be considered a simple question, the Buddha tried a different approach: "Perhaps you do not ask your questions out of respect for the teacher. Let one companion tell another his question."[292] This would allow individual monks to disassociate themselves from the question. Today's equivalent would be: "A friend, actually me, is confused about…" Still no questions from the monks.

Ananda exclaimed to the Buddha: "This is remarkable, sir, this is extraordinary---such is my confidence in the Blessed One: there is not a single monk in this community who has doubt or is confused about the Buddha, the teaching, the community, the path or the practice."[293] The Buddha corrected Ananda, pointing out that he could not know for certain that no monk had any doubts. Maybe a monk did not want to voice his insecurities in front of the other monks. And a question could arise later that a monk was not aware of now.

After explaining how Ananda had based his opinion on faulty reasoning, the Buddha then agreed with Ananda, but contrasted Ananda's emotional confidence with his enlightened insight: "you say this out of deep faith, Ananda. The Tathagata has knowledge of this: there is not a single monk in this community who has doubt or is confused about the Buddha, the teaching, the community, the path, or the practice. For the least of these five hundred monks has entered the stream and is beyond affliction, destined to full awakening for sure."[294]

It might seem unlikely that all five hundred monks totally understood; but the Buddha was able to use his extraordinary ability to enter others' minds to confirm the monks' understanding. Why, then, did he ask them if they had any questions? All he had to do was read their minds. Above all, it was a thoughtful and loving gesture by the sangha to reassure the Buddha in his final moments of life that they all understood; that he had taught them well.

The Buddha's final words were addressed to Ananda and the disciples: "Therefore, O Ananda, be lamps unto yourselves. Betake yourselves to no external refuge. Hold fast as a refuge to the truth.

Work out your own salvation with diligence."[295] An alternative final quote, with the same basic message, is: "Now, monks, I declare this to you: It is the nature of all conditioned things to vanish. Strive for the goal with diligence."[296]

The Buddha told his disciples that he had not held anything back in a clenched fist. They had everything they needed to reach enlightenment. But they had to use the Noble Eightfold Path in their everyday lives to apply the principles he taught. Then, the Dhamma would "become a living part of the believer, until he is no longer a follower, but a light unto himself."[297]

The speed of the Buddha's parinirvanization increased. He entered the stage of cessation of perception and feeling. Ananda misinterpreted the Buddha's stillness and remarked to Anuruddha: "The Blessed One has attained final Nibbana, venerable sir." Anuruddha and Ananda were cousins and had been ordained on the same day. Now, however, Anuruddha was a senior monk, an arhat; and he corrected Ananda: "The Buddha is in the state of cessation but has not yet passed away."[298]

The Buddha continued through the stages of concentration until, during the fourth jhana, at the age of eighty in 486 B.C.E.[299]the Buddha became parinirvanized---completely extinguished. "And when the Blessed One[300] attained final peace, with his final nibbana, the earth quaked, frightening, making the hairs stand on end, and claps of thunder rent the sky."[301] The two sala trees rained down "blossoms upon the Buddha's body" and the gods mourned.[302]

Ananda was beside himself with grief: "Then there was terror, and the hair stood up, when he, the all-accomplished one, the Buddha, passed away."[303]Some of the other unenlightened monks "...who had not yet got rid of greed spread their arms wide and called out; they fell to the ground, broken, and rolled back and forth."[304]

Anurhudda stepped up, took control of the situation, and gently, but firmly, reminded the sangha: "Enough sirs. Do not grieve and lament. Has not the Blessed One warned you about this before: We must lose and be deprived of and separated from everything pleasant and dear? So how else could it be? That something is born, come into being, conditioned, and of a nature to decay should not decay---this cannot happen. Sirs, the gods disapprove."[305]

Ananda and a select group of monks had witnessed the parinirvanization of the only Buddha who will appear in our age. Ananda had no stirring words to memorialize the Master. Instead, he asked an odd question: "But what sorts of gods does the venerable Anuruddha have in mind?" The sentence structure---"what sorts of gods" and "have in mind" is very informal and incongruous to the momentous historical event that had just occurred in his presence.

Translation could be a factor; but considering that Anuruddha was his superior, Ananda's question seemed flippant, sarcastic, and disrespectful. Did it indicate many years of competition and jealousy between the two? Ananda again evidenced a stark inability to understand even basic Buddhist theology, in this case the realms of existence. Another explanation is that Ananda could have been in shock. He had served his friend and mentor for twenty-five years. Now, in Ananda's unenlightened mind, the Buddha was dead---gone forever. Perhaps Ananda simply did not understand what just happened.

Anuruddha patiently explained the realms, including gods and demi-gods, to Ananda while comforting the other unenlightened monks and speaking with the assembled arhats. Then, for the rest of the night, Anuruddha and Ananda discussed the dharma. They had known each other all their lives and had served together as homeless beggars for forty-three years in the sangha, but "not a single conversation about the Dhamma seems to have taken place between these two very dissimilar siblings."[306]

In the morning, when their discussion concluded, Anuruddha told Ananda to go to Kusinara and tell the Mallas that the Buddha had attained final nibbana. This is an important moment in Ananda's life. Just twenty-four hours ago, he might have been outranked by the arhats, but he reported only to the Buddha. Now, the Buddha parinirvanized; and Ananda fell under the direct authority of the senior, enlightened arhats, including his cousin, whom he was to address as venerable sir. Whether Ananda felt any resentment about the situation is not recorded; but it is noteworthy that he replied "yes, sir" to Anurhudda;

not "yes, venerable sir" as the Buddha had instructed. Perhaps it was just too much, too soon for Ananda to accept the changes.

Ananda became the defacto organizer for the Buddha's funeral arrangements. Ananda followed Anuruddha's orders and informed the Mallas. As was apparently their custom when receiving bad news, the Mallas cried out, beat their breasts, fell to the ground, and rolled back and forth with disheveled hair. After the Mallas regained their composure, Ananda went over the steps involved in the intricate funeral ceremony.

At some point, while the complex funeral was being planned, Ananda returned to the Jetavana monastery. He found the monks and surrounding community in deep mourning. Ananda delivered a sermon to comfort them. He addressed the sangha "as if the Buddha were still in residence."[307] Then, probably to assuage his own grief, he threw himself into his daily routine of serving the Buddha. He changed the garlands, swept the floor of the Buddha's room, and performed other duties. The monk Buddaghosa commented that these actions showed Ananda's love for the Buddha, but they also proved that Ananda was "not yet free of passions."[308]

For six days, as the Buddha was lying in state between the two sala trees, humans and gods came to pay their respects. Ananda organized the event, and his duties were comparable to a modern-day funeral home director. He greeted dignitaries, monks, and locals. He kept the line of mourners who came to view the Buddha's body moving at a steady pace.

Large groups of Mallas arrived to venerate the Buddha's body. Ananda realized the Malla women at the back of the crowd could not see the Buddha, so he motioned for them to come to the front. "They break into lamentations, circumambulate the corpse, and make all sorts of offerings to it, except for one old widow who has nothing to give. Carried away with emotion, she bursts out crying, and her tears run down and wet the Buddha's feet."[309]

Kasyapa, the Buddha's chief disciple and Ananda's foe, was on-the-road preaching and did not find out about the Buddha's parinirvanization until a week later. He started the journey to Kusinagari to pay his respects. Meanwhile, the Mallas concluded their veneration of the Buddha's corpse "and have now shrouded it in a thousand layers of cloth and encoffined it in its iron sarcophagus."[310]

On the seventh day, the Buddha's body was to be transported through the city to the cremation site. But Malla tradition held that the city would be defiled if a corpse was carried through it. When they tried to lift the coffin to carry it outside the city limits to the funeral pyre, it would not move. Anuruddha explained that the gods watching the ceremony wanted the Buddha to be carried through the city. The Mallas agreed and "the corpse moved easily, and the heaven rained flowers."[311] The Mallas concluded that, unlike regular corpses, the Buddha's body was pure.

The pre-cremation was a wild scene. The Mallas tried and failed to light the cremation fire. Anruddha said the gods were preventing it until Kasyapa arrived so he could see the Buddha's body. Supernatural explanations aside, there is also the possibility that the iron sarcophagus could have retarded the fire's ignition.

Kasyapa finally arrived with five hundred monks and was angered to discover that Ananda had broken protocol by allowing women to see the Buddha's body before Kasyapa and the arhats.[312] This serious breach of protocol would later be brought up at Ananda's trial. Then, spectators were shocked when the Buddha's feet suddenly shot out of the iron coffin, allowing Kasyapa to venerate them. It is not clear whether the gods moved the Buddha's feet or if the Buddha moved them post-parinirvana or if Kasyapa simply pulled on them.[313]

In another story, the Buddha's mother, Queen Mahamaya, is in Tusita heaven and is informed of the Buddha's parinirvanization. When she comes down to mourn her son, the coffin lid magically opens and the Buddha sits up and talks with his mother and Ananda: "He then tells his mother not to be overwhelmed by grief, that his passing away is in harmony with the law of all things, and that even with his extinction, there are still the refuges of the dharma and the sangha." The Buddha closes this extraordinary soliloquy by telling Ananda his short sermon was a "lesson in proper filial conduct."[314]

The bad blood between Kasyapa and Ananda only intensified

when, after talking with Ananda, the Buddha then stuck his hand out of the coffin and waved goodbye to Ananda.[315] All the Buddha did for Kasyapa was thrust his feet out of the casket for Kasyapa to venerate. Kasyapa was angry and embarrassed and jealous. Later, when Kasyapa presided over the first Buddhist council, he made sure Ananda was charged with violating protocol.

When the drama of the Buddha's veneration subsided, the funeral pyre spontaneously combusted---"caught fire of itself"[316] and the Buddha's "beautiful body"[317] was totally consumed, leaving "neither skin, under-skin, flesh, sinew, or joint-fluid."[318] No ashes or soot remained; only the Buddha's relics (bones). The cremation ceremony lasted seven days; until "streams of rain extinguished the flames, and the Mallas took the bones to their council hall."[319] They displayed the remains, surrounded by a "hedge of spears and a fence of bows and honored them with dance and offerings of garlands and perfumes."[320] "for seven days"[321] After twenty-one days of veneration, the relics were divided into eight parts and eight stupas were built to house them.[322]

8

The First Council Is Planned

The Buddha's parnirvanization was a serious test for the senior monks in the Order. The rivalries and power struggles in the sangha that the Buddha had struggled to control were now in the open. Just one week after the Buddha's parinirvanization, elder Mahakassapa heard arhat Subhadda give a speech to the assembled monks. Earlier, the weak, but still commanding Buddha overruled Ananda's objections and agreed to answer questions that Subhadda had about Buddhism. Subhadda, who had been so interested in learning from the Buddha a week ago, now seemed to coldly dismiss the Master: "Surely, friends, do not grieve, do not lament, it's good riddance for us. We were annoyed by that great ascetic, who told us what is proper and is not proper. Now we can do what we wish to do and not do what we don't wish to do."[323]

Subhadda's attack on the Buddha seems particularly vicious and unnecessary. The Buddha was in his final moments of life; but he helped Subhadda overcome his obstacles to enlightenment; allowing Sudhadda to quickly become an arhat. Subhadda was the last of the Buddha's great disciples. He could have been a respected elder. Why did he turn on the Buddha and disparage him?

This is another example of a senior monk, an arhat, who is supposedly enlightened, exhibiting very little enlightened behavior. The account of this incident notes that Sudhadda "had become a monk in old age."[324] The relevance of Subhadda's age is not immediately clear, unless the chronicler intended to lessen the sting of Sudhadda's comments by inferring, perhaps, that Sudhadda was old and addled and did not understand what he was saying. It also should be noted that Ananda tried to prevent Subhadda from talking with the Buddha. Perhaps Ananda had a better insight into people's true motives than the Buddha. Ananda might have sensed Subhadda's treachery and was trying to protect the Buddha.

Whether he understood the significance of his words or not, Subhadda was suggesting that the sangha's successful discipline and structure instituted by the Buddha should now be abandoned. Kassapa knew if Subhadda's point-of-view was adopted, it would be the end of the Order.[325] The sangha was being weakened by these internal battles. Kassapa mulled over the remarks by Subhadda and saw that an official, authentic record of the Dhamma and Vinaya had to be established as-soon-as-possible to save the Order:

> This setting which now exists is one where evil monks
> think 'this word is from a teacher who has passed away,'
> and when they get followers, the true *dhamma* may
> disappear quickly. As long as the *dhamma* and *vinaya*
> exist, there will be the word of a teacher who has not
> passed away. Since the Blessed One said, 'Oh Ananda,
> the *dhamma* and the *vinaya* that I have taught and made
> known to you will be your teacher after my death,'
> what if I should recite the *dhamma* and the *vinaya* so
> that this sasana [teaching] will last for a long time and be
> perpetual?[326]

Kassapa, now confident about what needed to be done, gave a rousing speech to the assembled monks. He urged a back-to-basics approach to the Dhamma and Vinaya:

Let us friends, recite the Dhamma and the Vinaya.
Formerly what is contrary to the Dhamma shined
and Dhamma was disregarded, formerly what is
contrary to Vinaya shined and Vinaya was disregarded,
formerly those who held views contrary to Dhamma
were powerful and those who professed the Dhamma
were weak, formerly those who held views contrary
to Vinaya were strong and those who professed Vinaya
were weak.[327]

Kassapa was urging the Order to simply embrace the Buddha's teachings. The monks agreed: "In that case, sir, may you pick elder monks."[328] The Order was at the edge of a precipice. Kassapa had to move fast. He needed serious, tradition-oriented monks to codify and authenticate the Buddha's teachings (Dhamma) and to set down specific rules and regulations (Vinaya.) for managing the sangha. It is not an exaggeration to say that the future of Buddhism as a viable religion depended upon Kassapa's wisdom in choosing which monks would attend the first council.

Reports vary on when the first council was held. Some historians say it occurred sometime "less than a year after the Buddha's parinirvanization.[329] Other accounts report that "It was held on the full moon day of the month of Bhaddapada during the rainy season, four months after the death of the Lord, which occurred on the day of the festival of the full moon in the month of Visakha."[330] And, other sources say the First Council was held as soon as three months after the Buddha's departure.[331]

Ananda's enemies took advantage of the turmoil in the sangha to strike at him. Many enlightened monks had always been wary of Ananda. They knew he was not enlightened and, frankly, they did not trust him. Of course, there is no enlightenment exam. One's thoughts and actions are the only clues. Some of the arhats openly questioned Ananda's qualifications to participate in the meetings. There was also a large amount of jealousy among arhats concerning Ananda's access to the Buddha.

As the pre-council discussions were going on, in small clusters of monks throughout the meeting area, Ananda told a group of Bhikshus about a conversation he had with Sariputra and Maha-maudgalyayana while they were all staying in Sravasti. The two senior monks approached him with a serious question. The conversation probably took place several months before the Buddha became parinirvanized, since Ananda is described as having been the Buddha's attendant for twenty-five years and Sariputra died a month before the Buddha. The tense exchange reveals the simmering tension between Ananda and some of the senior monks.

The purpose of the conversation could have been the aged Sariputra's attempt to extinguish any remaining attachments as his nirvana approached. The apparent anger and resentment Sariputra held toward Ananda was certainly an attachment that would have to be extinguished or Sariputra's parinirvana would not occur. Ananda recounted the conversation.

> *Sariputra*: "Ananda, O wisest one, you have attended Buddha for twenty-five years. We wonder if, during that time, you have had any desires in your mind."
> *Ananda:* "My venerable Sariputra. I am as one who is still learning."

Sariputra repeated the same question "over and over again," and Ananda always responded, "I am as one who is still learning."

> "Ananda, I am not asking you if you are one still learning; or whether you have no more to learn; but if, whether during these twenty-five years, you have had any desires or not."

Again, Ananda answered: "I am as one who is still learning."

Finally, the clearly frustrated Maha-Maugalyayana delivered a sharp rebuke intended to put Ananda in his place. "Ananda, you should answer exactly and quickly. You should not act with obstinance toward your superior."

The superior remark, obviously intended to intimidate Ananda, did not have its desired effect, because Ananda coolly replied "Oh, Sariputra, I could not, while living so close to Buddha, have desire for any thing. It is always so. One constantly in the presence of those who are wise and pure cannot but be free from desires."[332]

For whatever reason, Ananda did not defend himself with the obvious reply: His total devotion to serving the Buddha for twenty-five years left him little time and energy to meditate and concentrate on enlightenment.[333] The long history of friction between Ananda and the senior monks made it doubtful, however, that the arhats would have accepted this excuse. Instead, Ananda's convoluted response sounds more like the non-reply of a present-day politician who answers in talking points, filled with generalities and platitudes, when confronted with a tough question.

The first part of Ananda's reply, "Oh Sariputra, I could not, while living so close to Buddha, have desire for any thing" reminded his jealous superiors that they might officially out-rank him, but he was "living so close to Buddha" every day. In other words: Ananda had the real power, not they.

Did Ananda mean that he controlled his desires only while he was in the presence of the Buddha? And Ananda said he had no desire for any thing, not any person. In English, putting a space between "any" and "thing" indicates that the speaker is talking about a particular "thing." However, "anything," with no space, means "any object, occurrence, or matter whatever." In a sense, "anything" means "everything" and "any thing" means a specific inanimate object or occurrence. This discrepancy could merely be a translation anomaly, but it adds credibility to Ananda's ability to outwit his opponents in the sanga.

In the last sentence, "It is always so. One constantly in the presence of those who are wise and pure cannot but be free from desires," Ananda again reminded Sariputra and Maha-Maugalyayana of his daily access to the Buddha. He then immediately pivoted to praise the Buddha. The subtle message was: "I was in the Buddha's presence every day. The Buddha would have known if I had desires. Are you questioning the Buddha's abilities?"

The following statement by Ananda appears to be a retelling of the above incident with Sariputra and Maha-Maugalyayana, but there is no indication of the actual date it occurred.

> Through the full twenty-five years
> That I have been in training,
> No sensual perception has arisen in me:
> See the excellence of the Dhamma!
> Through the full twenty-five years
> That I have been in higher training,
> No perception of hate has arisen in me:
> See the excellence of the Dhamma![334]

When Ananda says he was in training, he meant that he was a learner or a trainee on the road to enlightenment. It is important to always remember that Ananda was not enlightened. He had not extinguished the fetters of desire and attachment. This could have made his position as the Buddha's attendant problematic. Many of the arhats believed the Awakened One must have a servant who has also loosed the chains of attachment. Hence, their disdain of Ananda.

Ananda tried to compensate for this obvious weakness by claiming that "no thoughts of lust or hate arose in him because "his close connection with the Buddha and his devotion to him gave no room for these."[335] However, being close to enlightenment is not an equal substitute for actual enlightenment. The fires of desire and attachment can be tamped down temporarily through willpower, but if they are not doused forever with the water of enlightenment, the still-hot coals can ignite if the right tinder is added. The result could be a disastrous blaze of desire.

It is not recorded how the two senior monks reacted to Ananda's reply. His obfuscation, however, indicates his attempt to dodge a truthful answer. It had to have been obvious for many years to all enlightened monks that Ananda was not enlightened. Predictably, some of them held great resentment concerning the access this unenlightened monk had to the Buddha. Ananda also used a clever public relations strategy of inoculation. Since he told his supporters the events first, with his spin, they would not be shocked or surprised if his rivals later related the story.

This event begs the obvious question: Since jealousy and resentment are major obstacles to enlightenment, were Sariputra and Maha-Maugalyayana enlightened? A truly enlightened monk, who had cleansed himself of all desires and attachments, would not have entertained even a brief negative thought about Ananda. It is ironic that Maha-Maugalyayana, who actively recruited Ananda to accept the attendant position for the Buddha, later became a fierce rival of Ananda. One wonders what occurred between the two men to cause such a major rift.

Shortly after the Buddha's parinirvanization, in a serious blunder, Ananda took thirty of his young disciples on a walking tour. Unfortunately, the young men immediately walked away, and the sangha lost thirty promising initiates. Furious at Ananda's apparent incompetence, Kassapa sternly admonished Ananda for not properly guarding the brand-new disciples "while they were still unrestrained in the senses, immoderate in eating, not devoted to wakefulness."[336]

Kassapa accused Ananda of being a "trampler of the corn, a spoiler of families, whose followers are breaking away."[337] And, in what Kassapa probably considered the coup de grace for Ananda's influence in the sangha, Kassapa declared, "This youngster truly does not know his own measure."[338]

What was Ananda's defense to the substantive, serious charges of overestimating the commitment of his young disciples, failing to guard them properly, and letting them just walk away? He simply ignored those accusations. Instead, he quibbled that, since he had gray hairs on his head, it was not accurate to call him a youngster. Ananda effectively used wit to weaken Kassapa's valid criticisms.

The youngster description of Ananda also corroborates accounts that Ananda was much younger than the Buddha and most of the arhats. This event and others indicate that Ananda's brain might also have moved a bit quicker than the average arhat. It appears that one of the side effects of enlightenment might be losing one's sense of humor. Ananda's verbal nimbleness and effective use of wit usually allowed him to talk his way out of difficulties. Then, everything changed. The Buddha became parinirvanized and Ananda lost his protector.

Even the Buddha, in his deathbed policy requiring that the sangha be operated according to seniority, seemed to desert Ananda. Some arhats no longer felt obligated to soften their criticisms of Ananda out of respect for the Buddha. Now they openly expressed their distain of Ananda. The boiling point was reached immediately following the Buddha's parinirvanization, when the First Buddhist Council was held to discuss the future of the Buddhist community. Mahakasyapa led five hundred arhats who gathered for the council. All were enlightened except Ananda.[339] This was a serious problem. Ananda had memorized most of the Buddha's discourses. He knew more than most of the arhats, but the fact remained: Ananda had "only reached the first stage of sainthood, Sotapanna"[340]He was not enlightened and so was not considered an equal by the arhats.

Ananda's description of his service to the Buddha probably damaged his case. It was powerful and heart-felt, but it only amplified the perception that Ananda was just the Buddha's servant...and unenlightened:

> For twenty-five years I served the Blessed One,
> I served him well with loving deeds
> Like a shadow that does not depart.
> For twenty-five years, I served the Blessed One,
> I served him well with loving speech
> Like a shadow that does not depart.
> For twenty-five years I served the Blessed One,
> I served him well with loving thoughts
> Like a shadow that does not depart.[341]

Ananda's speech did not seem to impress many of the enlightened monks. It must have sounded like Ananda was applying for a job. Ananda repeated six times that he served the Buddha. An arhat is not a servant. An arhat "has fully transcended all passion and desire to at last enjoy the cool bliss of Nirvana. They do not manufacture any new karmic formations, but old ones still have to be worked out and through their momentum mundane life persists, though they put their remaining time in the world to good effect by teaching the Dhamma."[342] They too are enlightened, just like the Buddha. They felt they were the Buddha's equal. The primary difference is that the Buddha earned his enlightenment by self-discovery and arhats were taught by a Buddha. It is certain that none of the arhats felt they were the Buddha's servants.

Although Buddhism did not consider the caste of prospective monks, ironically, the sangha itself segregated monks according to their level of wakefulness: from stream-enterers, once-returners, and non-returners on the path to enlightenment to the final step of an enlightened arhat. This strict hierarchy in the sangha immediately emerged as a serious problem in planning the Council. The question was: Should only arhats be allowed to attend the Council?

It was clear which monks were enlightened and which were not. "The Enlightened disciples understood that all things are impermanent, while the unenlightened grieved at the loss of the Bhagavan, the Blessed One."[343] A truly enlightened monk would have understood that the Buddha had achieved what they were all working toward: nirvana. It was a joyous event, not a time to grieve.

Some arhats believed that, since Ananda openly wept as the Buddha was entering nirvana, Ananda showed attachment to the Buddha and, thus, was not enlightened. Some senior monks insisted that Ananda not be allowed to participate in the proceedings and several even suggested that Ananda be barred from attending the council even as a mere spectator.

This was the perfect opportunity for Ananda's detractors to attack. The earlier encounter between Ananda, Sariputra, and Maha-maudgalyayana became an important factor by setting the stage for a bitter confrontation between two opposing groups. On one side, a faction of arhats opposed Ananda's participation unless he reached enlightenment before the first meeting. His supporters reminded the group that Ananda had been the Buddha's companion and caregiver for twenty-five years. He had heard and memorized more of the Buddha's Sutras than any other disciple. *Ergo:* Ananda must be heard, for the good of the Order, regardless of whether he was enlightened.

When the date for the council was agreed upon, the Venerable Anu-Ruddha, Ananda's cousin and half-brother, suggested that, despite Ananda's encyclopedic knowledge of the Buddha's Sutras, Ananda should not be admitted to the council unless he successfully broke his remaining fetters and attained arahantship before the first meeting. That proposal was approved by the group.

Kassapa was then asked to choose the members of the council. He "selected five hundred elders all but one of whom were arahants."[344] The final chair was left open for Ananda; just in case he could achieve enlightenment before the council met. It is fair to say that Kassapa and Ananda were not close friends. They were fierce rivals in the sangha. But Kassapa knew Ananda's participation at the council was crucial. Without his perfect memory of the Buddha's discourses, the future of the Order would be in peril. Like the Buddha, Kassapa would do whatever was necessary to preserve the Order.

This hard deadline was apparently the motivation Ananda needed. He buckled down and worked diligently on achieving enlightenment. Kassapa recommended that Ananda live in the forest near Kosala so he would have quiet and solitude. Unfortunately, when the locals found out Ananda was there, he was inundated with visitors who treated him like a celebrity. They asked about the Buddha, Sariputra, Moggallana, and King Pasenadi, who had all died within the last year.[345]

Ananda did his best to comfort the visitors and gawkers, but his focus on enlightenment became scattered. He needed peace and quiet; but he was never alone. It was impossible to concentrate. He spent most of his days and nights consoling the lay disciples. Finally, a forest deity, who was worried that the frenetic activity was interfering in Ananda's studies appeared and said "Having entered the thicket at the foot of a tree, Having placed Nibbana in your heart, Meditate, Gotama, and be not negligent! What will this hullabaloo do for you?[346]

That pep-talk from the deity energized Ananda and he threw himself into meditation. The pressure was on. If Ananda expected to attend the first council and have a role in shaping Buddhism's future, he would have to attain enlightenment.

9

The First Council

King Ajatasattu agreed to let the First Council to be held in Rajagaha.[347] "With Kassapa presiding, this Council rehearsed and committed to memory all that was known about the Buddha's teaching."[348] Kassapa served as the questioner, the interlocutor, while Upali covered the Buddha's rules of conduct. "Because Ananda, the Buddha's closest companion, was not yet acknowledged as an arhat, he was not invited to be part of the council. However, he was asked to recite Shakyamuni's sermons to the other members. "[349]

Ananda's intense quest for enlightenment is an exciting story of a race to the finish line. The night before the opening of the First Council, Ananda practiced intense mindfulness. "As he was preparing to lie down after a full night of striving, just when he had raised his legs off the ground but had not yet laid his head on the pillow, his mind was released from all cankers."[350] Ananda was enlightened in a flash![351]

Although historians agree that Ananda did not achieve enlightenment until the Buddha's parinirvanization, there are conflicting accounts on whether it occurred before or during the first council. Lee asserts that Ananda attained enlightenment the day before the first council[352] and Hecker says Ananda was enlightened on the first day of the first council;[353] so both accounts fit the historical data

Ironically, while the arhats were arguing over Ananda's non-enlightenment, he might have been achieving enlightenment. His supporters had set aside a seat for him in the Council meeting room, in the presumably dim hope that he might attain enlightenment before the first meeting. They were not disappointed. Ananda entered the meeting room, filled with more than five-hundred arhats, with a dramatic flourish. "Soon after all the other monks were seated Ananda arrived through the air by psychic power and sat down in his seat."[354]

Ananda's streak of showmanship by flying into the council could have gotten him into trouble. Earlier in the Buddha's ministry, a disciple named Pindola used his magical powers to levitate, so he could grab a sandalwood begging bowl that had been suspended at the top of a high pole. The Buddha reprimanded Pindola and, from that day forward, arhats were prohibited from ostentatious displays of their supernatural powers.[355]

So, by flying to his seat, Ananda broke one of the Buddha's rules; but no one seemed to mind. His spectacular entrance proved that he was indeed finally enlightened. The other arhats, including his detractors, "expressed their brotherly joy with him."[356] The council was declared open, and Ananda took his place as a full and enlightened member. But the disagreements and power struggles were far from over.

In a signal honor for Ananda, Kassapa "made Ananda sit upon the golden throne of the Buddha in the great temple in the stone grotto in Magadha, Central India, and repeat the teachings in the presence of the five hundred."[357] Ananda's masterly recitation of the "entire Sutra section of the Hinayana Tripitaka from memory"[358] commanded the respect of the arhats.

Ananda was truly an authority on the Buddha's discourses. "Uncorking a prodigious memory, he is said to have delivered verbatim every sermon the Buddha ever gave."[359] "He is said to have heard all 84,000 sermon topics (82,000 taught by the Buddha and 2,000 taught by other disciples) and was able to memorize 15,000 stanzas without omitting a syllable."[360]

The venerable Ajinata-Kaundinya was one of the five hundred arhats at the first council. His visceral, emotional reaction when he saw and heard Ananda recite the Buddha's Sutras can be better understood with some backstory. When the Buddha left his wife, Yasodhara, and son, Rahula, to seek enlightenment, he joined five aesthetics who believed extreme fasting would lead to nirvana. After six years of almost starving himself to death, the Buddha realized that extreme fasting was not only ineffective in reaching nirvana; it was very dangerous; so, he left the group and went out on his own.

Shortly after the Buddha was enlightened, he was walking down a road and met the five aesthetics. Initially, they were wary of him and agreed among themselves to snub him; but it soon became apparent that the Buddha had discovered something special, and they all became the Buddha's disciples. One of those aesthetics, who became one of the Buddha's first five disciples, was Ajinata-Kaundinya.

So, when Ajinata-Kaundinya saw Ananda sitting on the Buddha's throne and heard Ananda recite the Buddha's discourses, his reaction was immediate and visceral: "Ananda's voice, attitude, gesture, so faithfully portrayed the Buddha, that Kaundinya's old memories were recalled, so realistically, that he seemed to hear and see before him, his great teacher. Overcome with intense emotion, he fainted."[361]

The amazing aspect of this account is that Ananda recited the Buddha's discourses word-for-word, totally from memory. Ananda's accurate recitation, his uncanny grasp of the Buddha's personal mannerisms, and his ability to capture the Buddha's individual pronunciation, articulation, and emphasis of every word ever uttered by the Buddha was so true that a disciple who had known the Buddha probably longer than anyone was transported back in time and thought the Buddha was talking. The aged monk was so startled that he collapsed. This incident, more than any other, testifies to the genius of Ananda.

Other accounts praised Ananda's total recall of the Buddha's discourses and his astonishing ability to mimic the Buddha's voice and mannerisms. The elders at the first council were dumbfounded: "What? Is it possible? The Buddha has come back to earth and is still teaching! It is the Buddha whom we hear speaking thus!"[362] Today, some might say Ananda was channeling the Buddha.

When the Buddha was becoming parinirvanized, he was asked how future monks could identify his authentic thoughts, most of which had been memorized by Ananda. What should the initial words in a Sutra be? The Buddha answered: "For the initial line of all the Sutras, you must write, 'Thus I have heard.'"[363] This was a signal to the listener that Ananda was there. He saw and heard the Buddha say those exact words. The equivalent today would be a quote or a video soundbite. If "Thus I have heard" is not the opening line of a Sutra, it is not Buddhistic writing. Some texts translate the phrase as "Thus have I heard," but both indicate that Ananda heard the Buddha utter the words that follow.

The first council lasted seven months[364]in which the entire Sutra of the Buddha along with the rules and regulations for managing the sangha were spoken and memorized. Amazingly, the entire Buddhist canon (Sutra and Vinaya) was memorized and transmitted orally until they were committed to writing at "the fourth council held in Ceylon in about 80 BC"[365] The material was organized into three sections or baskets: the Vinaya/sangha rules; the Sutra/Buddha's discourses; and the Abhidamma/ philosophical and psychological development of the teaching.[366] These three baskets became known as the Tipitaka.

Ananda seemed to be winning over some of the skeptical arhats with his flawless recitation of the Buddha's Sutras. However, the animosity for Ananda held by some arhats began to surface. The sangha was entering a tumultuous period. Even after his enlightenment, Ananda was still not respected by some of his fellow arhats.

All of Ananda's past mistakes, failures in protocol, and personal slights were on Kassapa's mind when Ananda told the gathering that the Buddha told him the minor rules of conduct for the Sangha could be dropped. The problem was: Ananda did not ask the Buddha which rules he considered minor. Kassapa, frustrated by Ananda's failure to ask the Buddha to define the minor rules, suggested "it would be best not to abolish any of them. In that case we shall be sure that we are not acting contrary to the master's wishes."[367] So, just to be safe, all the rules were adopted for the ordained Sangha.[368]

At this point, several senior monks, led by Kassapa, confronted

Ananda, in what is commonly called the Trial of Ananda. They accused him of five serious breaches of discipline, judgment, and mindfulness by:

1. not asking the Buddha what the minor rules were.
2. sewing a robe for the Buddha after he had stepped on the cloth.
3. allowing women to view the Buddha's naked body before the arhats, resulting in their tears falling on his feet and discoloring his feet.
4. failing to ask the Buddha to live for the rest of the kalpa.
5. urging the Buddha to admit women to the Order.[369]

Kassapa was still upset that he was not present to witness the Buddha's parinirvanization. And he became incandescent with anger when monks began to relate the miraculous events claimed by Ananda while the Buddha was lying in state. Kassapa had had enough. He tried to finish off Ananda's influence in the sangha by accusing Ananda of negligence of duty.

For example, when Kassapa came to venerate the Buddha's feet, he immediately noticed the discoloration caused by the old woman's tears. Kassapa accused Ananda of breach of protocol because an unenlightened old peasant lady got to revere the Buddha's corpse before Kassapa, the Buddha's chief disciple, had the chance. Kassapa added another very serious charge. Ananda had allowed the Malla women to see the Buddha's "sheath-encased penis." The arhats demanded Ananda confess his wrongdoing.

The animosity between Ananda and the senior monks is evident in his replies. "He submitted to the judgment of the other elders, although he himself could not see any wrongdoing, a fact that he did not fail to mention."[370] A different account reached the same conclusion: "Ananda replied that he saw no fault in any of these deeds but agreed to confess them." [371] Ananda's strategy could be compared to an Alford plea or best interests plea in today's judicial system in which the defendant maintains his innocence but admits that the prosecution probably has enough evidence for a conviction at trial.

Ananda apparently decided to admit mistakes that he considered to be merely insignificant oversights. He grudgingly accepted the blame for not getting the minor rules defined and said he meant no disrespect to the Buddha when he accidentally stepped on the Buddha's robe. He said he allowed the Malla women to pay homage to the Buddha early because he was concerned for their safety. He wanted to be sure they could get home before dark. And he allowed the women to see the Buddha's penis so they would be ashamed of their female bodies and would work diligently in this life so they could be reborn as men. Scholars also note that the Buddha's corpse had been washed. By tradition, in India, female relatives of the deceased usually did that task; so, it would not have been unusual for women to see the Buddha's naked body.[372]

Ananda did not have a strong defense for the most serious charge of not asking the Buddha to extend his life. Ananda's job was to listen closely to the Buddha, so Ananda should have been more mindful. Lawyers joke that when the law is on your side, you argue the law. When the facts are on your side, you argue the facts. But when you don't have the law or the facts on your side, you just argue and pound the table. Ananda's defense was in that vein, although, presumably, he did not pound the table. He said he did not ask the Buddha to extend his life because he had been possessed by Mara. Ananda told the elders that interference by Mara was the only possible explanation for him failing in his duty.

A cursory analysis of the above infractions shows one that stands out. One that fundamentally changed the sangha. One that enraged the heretofore all-male membership. The admission of women into the Order. There is no record of how or if Ananda even addressed that final complaint at his trial. "But partly because of his role in this controversial matter he came in for a great deal of criticism from some of his contemporaries and seems to have treated as a scapegoat or focus for the grievances of some of his fellow monks."[373] It is puzzling that senior, enlightened arhats might have believed that Ananda, an unenlightened monk, had such power over the Buddha. That charge feels like an attempt to pile on because it doesn't make sense.

In the end, the so-called trial of Ananda fizzled out. The Buddha's parinirvanization merely unleased the simmering jealousies of some of the arhats toward Ananda. He had faithfully served the Buddha and the sangha for twenty-five years, a long record of activities, but his accusers could not find any substantive charges that would stick. After verbal sparring and more than a little huffing and puffing by Ananda's detractors, the first council quickly returned to the enormous job of collating and organizing the Sutras and Vinayas.

10

Ananda's Twilight Years

After the Buddha's parinirvanization, the Venerable Mahakassapa (Kassapa) became the leader of the sangha. Kassapa was one of the Buddha's most revered and respected disciples, so his status as an elder meant that guidance of the Order naturally became his responsibility. Monks turned to Kassapa for all questions concerning the sangha. Ananda became the "second most venerated one."[374] At the age of one hundred, Kassapa retired and passed on the authority to lead the sangha to the fifty-year old Ananda. For the next seventy years, Ananda continued to travel and teach. Ananda continued to advise his fellow monks after the Buddha's parinirvanization. He slowly gained the respect of the senior monks, due to his prodigious memory of the Buddha's Sutras and his enlightenment.

Although Sariputra is a frequent critic of Ananda in many incidents, the two apparently "enjoyed a close friendship"[375] with each other. Sariputra died a few months before the Buddha and, even though he was enlightened, Ananda was never able to overcome the loss of these two friends. While other enlightened monks praised Buddha and Sariputra for eliminating samsara, Ananda seemed to understand parinirvana on an intellectual level, but he simply could not accept the physical absence of his close friends.

Ananda grieved the Buddha, his friend and Master, for the rest of his life. The following passages were written by Ananda when he was nearing his own parinirvana. They indicate the loneliness of old age and the gaping wound in Ananda's heart caused by the Buddha's absence that even enlightenment could not heal:

> All the directions are obscure,
> The teachings are not clear to me.
> With our benevolent friend gone,
> It seems as if all is darkness.
> For one whose friend has passed away,
> One whose teacher is gone for good,
> There is no friend that can compare
> With mindfulness of the body.
> The old ones have all passed away.
> I do not fit in with the new.
> And so today I muse alone
> Like a bird who has gone to roost.[376]

Buddhist dogma teaches that parinirvana is not death. It is a completely different realm of existence impossible to completely understand because the only words we can use to describe it are based on our perceptions of the temporary physical world. Although enlightened now, Ananda could not accept Buddha's parinirvanization. How can we expect to explain another dimension when we are trapped in the mire of desire and attachment all around us?

In his twilight years, Ananda lived in the woods of Magadha.[377] He was walking one day and heard a young monk incorrectly reciting a Sutra. Ananda stopped and tried to help the novice. There are varying accounts of what happened next. Some stories say the novice laughed at Ananda and said "O my venerable patriarch, you are in your dotage. My own teacher is highly enlightened, and he is young and keen of intellect. He instructs me most kindly, and I believe, there is no error in his teaching."[378] Others report that the monk's teacher said Ananda had gotten old and his memory was faulty. One can only hope that the brash young novice was so full of himself that he did not recognize the Venerable Ananda. A troubling question arises. If the

Sutras were misunderstood and distorted so soon after the Buddha's parinirvanization, how accurate are they today?

The young man's insulting treatment of the revered Ananda was devastating to a man who had been the Buddha's trusted hearer and friend. Ananda was so respected by the Buddha that, years earlier, when the Buddha was informed of Ananda's answers to questions about the dharma Ananda had given in the Buddha's absence, the Buddha replied:

> Ananda, monks, is wise, one of great understanding.
> If you had questioned me about this matter, I would
> have answered in the very same way that Ananda has
> answered. That is the meaning, and so you should
> bear it in mind.[379]

Could there be higher praise? At the first council, Ananda sat in the Buddha's chair and flawlessly recited the Buddha's discourses. The novice monk, in his youthful arrogance, was apparently oblivious to the fact that he was in the presence of a great man.

The disrespect was too much for the proud Ananda. He turned away silently and said to himself:

> I am full of years. I wished to live long to uphold Buddha's
> right teaching for the sake of all sentient beings; but their
> minds are covered with grime too thick and too hard to let
> them understand my love. It is of no profit to stay longer
> with them. Rather shall I enter into Nirvana and that
> quickly.[380]

Ananda decided then and there to enter final Nirvana at the age of 120.[381] While the Buddha's departure was quiet and dignified, surrounded by arhats and disciples, Ananda would enter parinirvana alone. But he had commitments to keep first. He had once promised King Ajasattu that he would let the King know when he was going to enter final nirvana. The King wanted to witness the event and secure Ananda's relics (ashes and bones), presumably to make sure Ananda's remains were treated with care and respect. So, Ananda sent word to King Ajasattu that he planned to achieve parinirvana in Vesali.

The day arrived. Ananda was in the River Ganges crossing north to Vaisali.[382] King Ajasattu arrived in an armoured carriage and posted his army on the south shore of the river to witness Ananda's final nirvana. Meanwhile, on the north side of the river, the king of Vaisali, also heavily armed, had gathered for the same reason. He "posted his army of a thousand men" along the north shore of the river. Thus, the two armies in full array opposed each other on the opposite sides of the river with weapons and flags, shadowing the sun."[383]

This was a very tense situation. Ananda realized that if he entered nirvana on either side of the river, one of the clans would surely be angry. "Ananda, reaching the middle of the river, observed this battle array, and feared that they would kill each other."[384]

Ananda had the solution. Always the diplomat, "Ananda levitated to the middle of the river in the meditative posture, preached the dharma, and then meditated on the Tejokasina."[385] Another report agrees that "at age 120, he entered final Nirvana at the River Ganges which ran between two cities to pacify a war." [386]As he ascended higher into the sky, he achieved parinirvana and, in what must have been a spectacular and terrifying sight, his body erupted into flames and his relics landed equally on both banks of the river. "And each king together with his whole army wailed, mourning the departure of Ananda; and each of the kings built a tall tower on his side of the river in his own country."[387]Ananda's choice of location, the middle of the river, for his parinirvana, is a not-so-subtle metaphor for the value of the middle way.

11

Conclusion

Ananda was pivotal in the spread of Buddhist philosophy. It is not an exaggeration to claim that Buddhism would not have flourished without Ananda's precise, accurate oral recitations of the Buddha's discourses. Ananda is praised as "the most widely loved" of all the Buddha's disciples. "If Sariputra personified wisdom and Moggallana personified psychic ability, then Ananda certainly personified kindness, gentleness, warmth and love."[388]

He is considered one of the Buddha's Ten Most Influential Disciples, even though the entire time he worked for the Buddha, at least twenty-five years, Ananda was not enlightened. There are numerous stories of men who heard the Buddha speak, joined the sangha, and immediately became enlightened. Not Ananda. He did not receive enlightenment until after the Buddha's death; which begs the question: Why did the Buddha retain Ananda as his attendant for so many years when the Buddha could have chosen any number of more qualified followers who had become enlightened? There are several logical reasons. Ananda was the Buddha's cousin. People haven't changed that much in two thousand five hundred years. The tendency to trust and confide in blood relatives is consistent through the ages. Ananda idolized the Buddha. Ananda was born the same year as the Buddha's son, Rahula. Ananda grew up hearing exciting stories about his older cousin's adventures. Ananda wanted the peace that the Buddha had achieved. They met early in the Buddha's ministry and Ananda joined the sangha.

Ananda comes through the Buddhist historical records as a blue-collar monk. For two thousand five hundred years, each generation has been able to identify with Ananda's struggles. Ananda's sole life purpose was to serve the Buddha. His dedication and loyalty to the Buddha was certainly a factor in his inability to attain enlightenment in the Buddha's lifetime. Ananda had a sharp mind with a disarming wit. Ananda is a sympathetic character because "he was not the wisest of the Buddha's disciples but showed unstinting devotion to the Buddha, always seeking to understand him correctly and to bring his teachings to as many people as possible."[389]

The triad of the Buddha, his son Rahula, and Ananda is an interesting case. The Buddha clearly respected Rahula, who was ordained into the sangha as a child and attained enlightenment at the age of only 18. Rahula was clearly a gifted monk and was part of the Buddha's inner circle. He is considered one of the Buddha's ten most influential disciples. But it appears that a close, familial bond was not adequately formed between them, perhaps due to their family history.

Siddhartha Gautama left to seek enlightenment when Rahula was a newborn. Fathers leaving their family in search of the truth was not particularly unusual in that age and since Siddhartha's family was rich, Rahula was well-taken care of. Siddhartha traveled extensively during his six-year quest and the records do not report him visiting his estranged family during that time. When the Buddha returned to Kapalivastu, Rahula was still a child, but the Buddha was enlightened and the opportunity to reignite the paternal love for Rahula had been extinguished in the Buddha. Likewise, Rahula joined the Sangha as a child and was soon enlightened, so both were not encumbered by emotion and desire.

If Ananda and Rahula are indeed the same age, the Buddha's fatherly relationship with Ananda takes on new meaning. Is Ananda the son that the Buddha left behind? Popular culture frequently describes parents who were very strict in the upbringing of their children, but become overly lenient with their grandchildren, presumably to make up for their past transgressions. The Buddha might have viewed Ananda as a second chance to salve the guilt he felt for leaving his wife and son many years earlier.

The Buddha also saw, in Ananda the downside, for lack of a better term, of attaining enlightenment. Giving up attachments includes giving up strong human feelings; the most powerful of which is love. The Buddha's perfect enlightenment could have hindered his understanding of common people if he had not had Ananda to keep him in touch with reality.

Ananda, in a sense, represented the unenlightened masses for the Buddha. Ananda's emotional reactions to situations might have aided the Buddha in preparing his Sutras. By watching Ananda's loving, dedicated service, the Buddha understood, in very human terms, the many sacrifices necessary for enlightenment because Ananda's strong love for and commitment to the Buddha was a major obstacle in Ananda's enlightenment.

The close bond between the Buddha and Ananda could be due, in part, to the age difference between them, the fact that they were cousins, Ananda's dedicated service to the Buddha, Ananda's incredible ability to hear and recite the Buddha's discourses, and, at a much deeper, psychological level, the Buddha's possible guilt for abandoning his wife and new-born son, Rahula, to seek enlightenment.

As the Buddha's parinirvanization grew closer, a follower found Ananda weeping. He brought Ananda to the Buddha, who comforted Ananda. An amazing scene: The Buddha, quickly entering parinirvanization, comforting the grieving Ananda. This account is a subtle reminder that enlightenment does not require the total abandonment of loving kindness. The key is to avoid an unhealthy attachment to any desire. The Middle-Way put to practical use.

The Buddha encouraged Ananda to keep working toward enlightenment, but he never seemed overly concerned that Ananda was not enlightened. From a purely strategic standpoint, in an age before writing, when memory and oral recitation was paramount, the Buddha depended upon Ananda's phenomenal ability to recall his teachings to inspire the sangha, recruit potential followers. and ensure the sangha's continuation. Thus, though unenlightened, Ananda's extraordinary gift of memorization might have had a much higher value to the Buddha than just another enlightened arhat.

Why did the Buddha choose Ananda to be his companion from among the large Sangha? As is common in all powerful people, the Buddha could be very demanding, and he had a low tolerance for mistakes. He advised against traveling with fools, so we must assume that he did not suffer fools gladly or at all if he could manage it. Ananda, though, committed serious blunders that probably would have resulted in any other monk being summarily sacked. But the Buddha seemed to have enormous patience with Ananda. Instances of the Buddha's gentleness with Ananda's mistakes were discussed earlier in this book. The Buddha had a soft spot for Ananda, who clearly idolized the Buddha. The deep personal connection between the cousins is evident.

Historical figures, particularly religious leaders, are too often portrayed as cardboard cutouts. They often seem lifeless because their function is to promulgate doctrines. Any humanity is squeezed out and replaced with a humorless, emotionless android who spouts stilted religious homilies. But all historical figures were human. They had desires. They had a sense of humor. After reading and analyzing the many conversations between the Buddha and Ananda, one can imagine the two men, late at night, after a long day of traveling and preaching, quietly, informally talking with each other as friends.

Ananda was respectful and subservient to the Buddha, but he was very proud of his service to the master: "For twenty-five years I served the Lord with loving deeds, loving words and loving thoughts — when the Buddha paced to and fro, I paced along behind." [390]

Ananda told an assembly of monks that he had received and memorized the entire catalog of the Buddha's discourses: "I received from the Buddha 82,000, And from the bhikkhus 2,000 more. Thus, there are 84,000 units. Teachings that are set in motion." [391]

Many years after Ananda started working for the Buddha, apparently at the first council, Ananda addressed the Bhiksus:

O all my wise brethren, for twenty-five years I have been the attendant of Buddha. I have never carried myself proudly because of that, for, had I felt self-esteem, I would never have been with the Buddha these many years. Though I have served Buddha since twenty-five years ago, I have never seen him except at the proper times of attending him.[392]

As Ananda continued, he got caught up in the moment:

I have never experienced blame from Buddha except once, when he blamed me because he could not blame me. I have received eighty thousand teachings from the Tathagata. I am still holding them in mind without forgetting them. If I had been filled with self-gratulation, today, I would not find myself in possession of this knowledge. I have received eighty thousand Dharmas from the Tathagata. Never did I ask any question twice, not even so much as by one word. I have received these eighty thousand Dharmas from no one but him. I received them not by asking, but simply as he gave them to me; and I am remembering them because they are his words and because the wise among you, my brethren, is desirous of the knowledge of how to control himself, of how to emancipate himself, and of how to attain Nirvana."[393]

Ananda's claim that he was criticized only once by the Buddha was not exactly accurate. Ananda apparently forgot about not asking the Buddha to extend his life, remarking that dependent arising was easy to understand, and other instances. But the usually humble, diffident Ananda was finally in the spotlight, and it is understandable that he might have exaggerated a bit. In Shakespeare's King Henry the Fifth, the king gave a rousing speech to his men before the upcoming battle. "He that shall live this day and see old age...will remember with advantages what feats he did that day."[394] Perhaps Ananda was remembering with advantages his loyal service to the Buddha.

Some background is necessary to put the following account into perspective. Long after Ananda's parinirvana, in the eighth century BCE, he was the subject of a Chinese text entitled <u>Sutra for the Spell that Brought Deliverance to the Flaming Mouth Hungry Ghost.</u> The hungry ghost realm is primarily inhabited by those who died unenlightened and were greedy, lustful, and miserly when they were humans. However, the following story relates how some spirits become hungry ghosts because their families have not made proper offerings to feed their departed relatives.

Ananda was meditating when a hungry ghost named Flaming Mouth appeared and said Ananda would die in three days and would be reborn as a hungry ghost. The visage of Flaming Mouth was terrifying, as was his prediction; but Ananda regained his wits momentarily and asked Flaming Mouth how he could avoid this calamity. Flaming Mouth told Ananda that, the next day, he must "distribute one bushel of food and drink to hundreds of thousands of ghosts and to hundreds of thousands of brahmins." Then, Ananda's lifespan would increase and Flaming Mouth, coincidentally, would be released from the Hungry Ghost realm to be reborn as a god.

When Flaming Mouth disappeared, Ananda realized it would be impossible to acquire that much food and feed all those people and ghosts in one day. The Buddha, of course, had the answer. He suggested that, if Ananda recited a specific, long, elaborate mantra, Flaming Mouth would be satisfied. This feeding of the hungry ghosts ritual lasts up to five hours and became the responsibility of monks and nuns.[395]

Ananda was a gentle, strong, intelligent, loyal friend and confidant to the Buddha. It is not hyperbole to suggest that Buddhism would not have gained traction and become the world's fourth largest religion, with an estimated three hundred fifty million adherents today, without the extraordinary memory and character of Ananda. He was the quintessential right man at the right time. To the Buddha, he truly was like a shadow that does not depart.

Appendix 1

A Brief Introduction to Buddhism

Ananda spent much of his life serving an extraordinary man. Siddhartha Gotama was the son of a tribal chieftain, a king of sorts, of a warrior clan. Siddhartha was born rich, protected, and pampered. He grew into a handsome young man, with many concubines. He was adept at fighting arts. By his teens, he had it all: money, women, alcohol, parties, the good life. But, in his mid-twenties he sensed that his life was empty of real meaning. At the age of twenty-nine, he gave up his plush lifestyle, his beautiful wife, and his newborn son to become a wandering ascetic, begging for meals, meditating, searching for the key to eternal happiness.

Siddhartha soon joined five other ascetics who believed that self-mortification, subjecting one's body to extreme suffering, would end suffering. For the next six years, he "limited his food and sleep, did not wash, lived naked or sky-clad is it was called,[396] often lived alone, and slept on beds of thorns in forests and charnel grounds. He held his breath until his head felt like it would explode, and he finally passed out. He roasted in the sun during the scorching Indian days and shivered from the cold at night. He "cut down on his food consumption so that he was eating only a few drops of soup a day."[397]

Siddhartha had tremendous will-power and he became the group's expert in all these hideous privations. But after six years of constant self-torture, Siddhartha came to two important realizations: (1) he was killing himself and (2) he was still no closer to enlightenment. His description of his slow, self-starvation is not for the squeamish:

> All my limbs became like the knotted joints of withered creepers, my buttocks like a bullock's hoof, my protruding backbone like a string of balls, my gaunt ribs like the crazy rafters of a tumble-down shed. My eyes lay deep in their sockets, their pupils sparkling like water in a deep well. As an unripe gourd shrivels and shrinks in a hot wind, so became my scalp. If I thought, 'I will touch the skin of my belly,' it was the skin of my backbone that I also took hold of, since the skin of my belly and back met. The hairs, rotting at the roots, fell away from my body when I stroked my limbs.[398]

The once glowing, golden skin of the handsome Siddhartha had become sallow. His athletic, muscular, warrior body was no longer strong and powerful. He now resembled a walking skeleton. Near death, he lost consciousness. In one account, a young woman named Sujata, who was tending her sheep, brought him some warm rice gruel, which undoubtedly saved his life. In a different version, two local women, Nanda and Nandabala, bring rice milk to Siddhartha.[399] The rice gruel or milk was a special recipe by the deities that would sustain Siddhartha for the next 49 days as he became the Buddha. During this seven-week period, Siddhartha did not eat, defecate, or bathe. The seven weeks is symbolically important because forty-nine days "is often said to be the length of time between death and rebirth."[400]

His five ascetic friends saw him take the food. Disgusted, they abandoned him, with the parting shot: "Gautama has taken to the easy life!" One wonders if those five ascetics who were so quick to judge Siddhartha were as dedicated as he to the extreme privations.

As Siddhartha slowly regained his strength, he realized that polar-opposite approaches to life were not successful. As a young Prince, his hedonism with wine, women, and song was not fulfilling. And the physical privations he endured with the ascetics only led to his suffering and near death, not enlightenment.

We all understand, on a basic level, that anything we desire so intensely that it becomes an obsession is unhealthy. But Buddhism clearly explains why. Any extreme desire creates psychological fetters or chains or cords that bind us to this physical plane of existence. Then, when we die, our minds are not free and clear, because the attachments we created in this life, through our desires, reel us back to the human realm or a lower or higher realm, forcing us to deal with the karma (actions) that our desires and attachments have created.

A fictional character from a blockbuster movie gives a concise definition of attachment. In Godfather III, Michael Corleone laments: "Just when I thought I was out...they pull me back in." Michael's attachment to violence and crime prevented him from moving beyond his criminal past; just as the desire for fame or money or power or a woman or a man or a car or anything in this world creates an attachment that delays our attainment of nirvana. We, like Michael Corleone, are pulled back to this existence by our desires and must suffer countless lifetimes of samsara.

Siddhartha continued his journey "seeking out other teachers, but finally became disillusioned by all their practices."[401] Then, he came upon a beautiful pipal tree, later called the Bodhi Tree, by a river near Bodh Gaya. He decided to make his stand there. He met a grass cutter who made him a seat.[402] Siddhartha sat under the tree and vowed that he would "not rise from this spot until I am enlightened. Flesh may wither away, blood may dry up, but until I gain enlightenment, I shall not move from this seat."[403] Indeed, Siddhartha sat motionless, silent, in deep meditation. Mara, the evil one, unsuccessfully tried every trick to distract him, ranging from "an army of terrible demons" to "bands of seductive nymphs."[404]

As he meditated, Siddhartha realized that moderation in all things is the key to eliminating the extreme desires that lead to attachment resulting in samsara. Although the Middle Way seems simple and intuitive, it was a revolutionary principle because it finally unraveled the core problem we all face. Siddhartha discovered how to eliminate the continuous, repeating cycle of death, rebirth, death, rebirth, death that we suffer by extinguishing the desires that keep us attached to this existence.

Siddhartha Gautama became the Buddha the night after he defeated Mara when he distilled his experiences into the Four Noble Truths and the Noble Eightfold Path.[405] Five weeks after the Buddha attained enlightenment, he traveled approximately 100 miles from Bodhgaya to Sarnath and encountered the five ascetics who had earlier deserted him.[406] On the full moon day of the Ashada month, he taught them the Dharma and they also became enlightened. This first discourse of the Buddha is known as "Turning the Wheel of the Dharma." The Order of Monks, the Bhikkhu sangha, was created. The sangha later grew to 60 Arahants and then, toward the end of the Buddha's ministry, to thousands.[407]

The Buddha taught that we experience countless cycles of birth-death-rebirth for thousands of lifetimes because we cling to the impermanent desires of this world. The Buddha discovered how we can cleanse ourselves of the impurities, desires, and attachments that keep us bound to this existence. If the precepts of the Noble Eightfold Path are assiduously followed, we can break the cycles of suffering brought about by samsara, achieve enlightenment, and reach nirvana.

The First Noble Truth, life is suffering, bluntly states what we all know, but don't say. It's important to stress that suffering is not necessarily intense physical pain. Any desire for anything, an expensive car, clothes, another person, money, power, creates suffering because if we don't get what we want, we suffer or if we get what we want, we still suffer because we want more. We suffer because we try to find happiness, contentment, and solace in our day-to-day lives, in this existence. The Buddha understood that we spend our entire lives chasing happiness in the visible world, but that isn't possible, because everything in this world is temporary.

We constantly seek a permanent happiness that is impossible to achieve, so we are struck in this existence by our unachievable desires. The Buddha discovered how to cleanse himself of the unwholesome roots, the fetters, that keep us bound to this world. The Buddha finally found the key to eternal bliss. He would never be reborn to suffer another lifetime because he had eliminated clinging to desires and emotional ties that condemn us to countless rebirths resulting in countless more suffering as we try to reach an impossible, unreachable, permanent happiness in this world. The Buddhist philosophy can be distilled into three words: nothing lasts forever.

Today, it seems that holy men have been replaced by television hucksters who promise us wealth and entrance to heaven if we'll just send them our money to seed the growth, so to speak. All our money really does is seed their bank accounts. The path to enlightenment is not a secret that we can only learn by giving away all our money to a shadowy cult. We don't have to pay for classes and pay for retreats and pay to advance through artificial levels of mindfulness that were created only to make more money for the creator. We don't have to pay someone who says the answer is in his "closed fist" and he'll open it for a certain amount of money. We don't have to pay for anything. We can just read and study and meditate and follow the Buddha's advice. And it's free.

With his final words, the Buddha emphasized that enlightenment does not depend upon belief in him or any specific person. He encouraged us not to accept any teaching based on trust. Personal experience is the only way to determine the validity of any religion. Experiment with Buddhist principles in your daily life. If the Four Noble Truths and the Noble Eightfold Path make your life better, adopt them. It's that simple. The Buddha showed us the path to freedom two thousand five hundred years ago—if we follow it.

The Four Noble Truths and the Noble Eightfold Path are the Buddha's gifts to us. The Buddha's promise then is still valid now.

He gave us a clear road to true happiness. It's a difficult road and, realistically, it will take most of us this lifetime and maybe several more to reach enlightenment. But the answer is here--- now, in front of us, not in a closed fist but in the outstretched, open hand of the Buddha.

Appendix 2

The Buddha's Ten Most Influential Disciples

- *Sariputra* aka *Upatissa: Foremost in Wisdom.* Born on the same day as Moggallana, another chief disciple of the Buddha. Sariputra gained enlightenment two weeks after he was ordained. Parinirvanized a few months before the Buddha.
- *Moggallana* aka *Maudgalyayana*: Foremost in Possessing Supernatural Powers. Became a monk the same day as Sariputra and was enlightened seven days later, while obtaining supernatural powers. The Buddha usually discouraged his followers from using their supernatural powers, but Moggallana used his powers to spread the Dharma, so the Buddha approved. Two weeks after Sariputra died peacefully at home, Moggallana had a violent end to his life. While walking on a path, he was crushed when two men on a hill above him pushed rocks onto him. The legend states that Moggallana did not use his supernatural powers to stop the rockslide, because he knew it was his karma. It is rumored that the Buddha's arch-rival Devadatta, was behind the murder of Moggallana.

- *Mahakasyapa* aka *Massapa* aka *Kasyapa*: *Foremost in Asceticism*. Gained enlightenment eight days after becoming a disciple. Mahakasyapa did not consider himself a good speaker, so he tried to be a role model as a Buddhist ascetic. Usually stood to the left of the Buddha, with Ananda on the right. When the Buddha parinirvanized, Mahakasyapa took over leadership of the sangha. He presided over the First Council, in which important rules and procedures were laid down. When Mahakasyapa was one hundred years old, he turned over leadership of the sangha to Ananda and is said to have traveled to the Himalayas, where Mahakasyapa intended to meditate inside a mountain for six-point-seven billion years until the next Buddha arrives. At that time, he will pass on the Buddha's robe and alms bowl to the new Buddha.
- *Subhuti*: *Foremost in Realizing Emptiness*. His parents became Buddhists and urged Subhuti to meet the Buddha. He did and became the Buddha's disciple. Subhuti was the exemplar of how an enlightened person would approach the complicated concept of emptiness (voidness).
- *Purna Maitrayani-Putra* aka *Purna*: *Foremost in Preaching the Law*. Enthusiastic disciple; Top master of preaching. Thought about the future of Buddhism and vigorously spread he Buddhist doctrine. No evidence that Purna attained enlightenment.
- *Katyayana* aka *Mahakatyayana*: *Foremost in Spreading the Dharma*. Achieved enlightenment shortly after he became a disciple. Very good speaker. The Buddha praised Katyayana's ability to truly understand and explain his lectures.
- *Anuradha*: *Foremost in Divine Insight*. Ananda and Anuradha, both cousins of the Buddha, became monks at the same time. Anuradha was a master of clairvoyance and mindfulness. Once, when the Buddha was delivering a sermon, Anuradha dozed off. The Buddha reprimanded him and Anuradha was so embarrassed that he vowed never to sleep again. He soon had physical problems and even when the Buddha urged him

to sleep, he refused. Anuradha eventually went blind, but he practiced diligently and achieved enlightenment. Not only did his regular sight return, but he was given the power of the Heavenly Eye, which allowed him to see into the heavens and to recognize truth.

- **Upali:** *Foremost in Observing the Precepts.* Upali was an untouchable, a person from the lowest caste in India. He was sickly, so his parents decided he would be a barber. Upali was well-liked and soon became the barber for the Sakya clan, which meant he cut the Buddha's hair. Once, while giving the Buddha a haircut, he hesitantly asked the Buddha if he could join the Sangha. He figured he didn't have a chance, since he was from a low caste, but the Buddha agreed. So as Upali was cutting the Buddha's hair, he became a disciple, and immediately outranked many princes who joined after him since monks were ranked according to when they joined the Sangha, not by caste. Upali later became an arhat. Upali was top master of Vinaya and was a powerful voice in the first council.

- **Rahula:** *Foremost for His High Standard of Discipline and Obedience* aka *Foremost in Esoteric Practices and Desire for Instruction of the Dharma.* When the Buddha was still Prince Siddhartha Gautama, he married his cousin Yosodhara when both were sixteen. Their only child, a son, was born when they were twenty-nine. Siddhartha named him Rahula, translated as fetters, "because this son of mine is going to be my greatest hindrance; he is going to be my greatest enemy. He will prevent me from going to the Himalayas. Love for him, attachment to him, will be my chains"[408] Rahula might have concluded at an early age, that, if he could not have his father's love, he would try at least to gain his respect. Rahula spent his life trying to make his absent father proud of him, not an uncommon practice in any culture or any time. Rahula joined the sangha at the age of seven and was the first novice monk from the Buddha's hometown. Rahula achieved enlightenment when he was eighteen. Rahula's admittance into the sangha and enlightenment at such a young age removed any possibility of an emotional reconciliation between Rahula and the Buddha; since both were enlightened and both had eliminated strong emotion from their lives. This relationship also helps explain the closeness between the Buddha and Ananda. Perhaps the Buddha used the unenlightened Ananda to make up for his lost time with Rahula, who passed away before the Buddha, Sariputra, and Moggallana.

- **Ananda:** *Foremost in Hearing the Teachings of Buddha.* Ananda and the Buddha were first cousins. He was the Buddha's attendant for twenty-five years until the Buddha's parinirvanization. Ananda heard more of the Buddha's discourses than anyone else. The Buddha ranked Ananda as foremost amongst his disciples in five respects; erudition, retentive memory, good behavior[409] steadfastness, and ministering care.[410] At the First Council, the Sutras were compiled based on Ananda's recollections. Every Sutra recalled by Ananda begins with the words "Thus have I heard." This alerts the hearer or reader that the words were spoken by the Buddha. Ananda entered parinirvana at the age of one hundred twenty.

Appendix 3

The Four Noble Truths

After dedicating himself to extreme ascetism for six years and nearly starving himself to death, the Buddha left the ascetics and began the search for a middle way to enlightenment. He sat under a Bodhi tree and vowed not to move until he achieved enlightenment. Through intense meditation, he had a momentous breakthrough. He realized that our lives are filled with pain and uneasiness because of desire. We want this or that or a bigger this or a smaller that. We are consumed by desires for physical objects in this material, physical world. But we can never truly be satisfied because everything is a combination of elements that eventually disintegrate. The temporal world we live in and everything in it is temporary. Everything has a use by date. Everything eventually decays. Unfortunately, we keep clinging to decaying mirages in the mistaken belief that they are permanent and will make us happy.

Then, when we die, the attachments and karma we accumulated in this life and previous lives cause us to be reborn into one of the realms and endure more suffering and clinging and unsatisfied, unfulfilled wants and needs. The Buddha discovered that our life is like a treadmill. We run and run and run after illusory sensory pleasures, but we go nowhere. We're never satisfied. The Buddha---the doctor---developed a medicine--- the Four Noble Truths---to treat this illness.

1. Life is suffering (dukkha).
2. The suffering is caused by desire.
3. The suffering can end.
4. There is a clear path to end suffering.

In the **First Noble Truth,** the Buddha, performing the function of a doctor, diagnoses the suffering or dukkha. The western concept of suffering is generally physical: a broken limb, a migraine, a headache. These are all quick, accurate examples of suffering; but dukkha also includes more subtle, psychological conditions that affect us every day such as feelings of confusion, dread, fear, anger, imperfection, and uneasiness. These lingering mental kleshas can be more vexing than physical pain. The Buddha illuminated what we already know but might not admit. We all live in a constant state of uneasiness. Dukkha has been compared to the uneven axle of a cart. The cart still moves and gets us through our daily obligations; but it's difficult to steer and the ride is uneven and distressing. Dukkha is the mental equivalent of a bumpy cart.

The Buddha explained the cause of this debilitating dukkha in the **Second Noble Truth**. We have profound, gnawing desires that eat away at us, creating a huge, gaping wound in our psyche that we try to heal unsuccessfully with shiny objects, such as the new car, the expensive jewelry or desirable people, the beautiful woman, or the handsome man. Of course, it never works. The wound in our lives cannot be healed with worldly things because everything in this world is temporary, impermanent, an illusion. All objects eventually disintegrate. All people get old and unwell and die. It's a fact. It can't be stopped. What can be stopped, however, is the desire, the thirst, the craving for things that are impermanent.

At the top of the list of clinging to impermanence is the self. Nothing is permanent, including us. Our desperate attempts to be different confound the truth that we really are not different at all. Humans are composites of billions of atoms and we'll all eventually return to the earth to be recycled into something that is equally temporary. My physical form is composed as an aggregate of atoms. A separate self is nowhere to be found.

At this point, the reader could be suffering from distress in learning that everything is impermanent. The job you have, the love you feel for your significant other, your bright, shiny teeth, your bright, shiny car are all temporary and will eventually disintegrate. This concept can be a real downer for those who are new to Buddhism. I, however, find it uplifting. When I have a bad day and nothing seems to go right, I understand that this negative situation is not forever. It will end. Conversely, when I walk through the forest in the fall and hear the leaves crackling and see the squirrels jumping from tree to tree and marvel at the beautiful blue sky, I am aware that this wonderful moment will end but, very importantly, it can return.

The Second Noble Truth names the cause of our suffering: desire. We all desire something or someone. But when we get that expensive home, we find that the roof leaks or it was built on a nuclear waste site. We find that the person we were so attracted to because of his or her success or intelligence or caring attitude is not like that. The cliché "be careful what you wish for" accurately describes the suffering of desire. It's never enough. John D. Rockefeller founded Standard Oil Company at the turn of the twentieth century. He holds the distinction of being the wealthiest American of all time and the richest person in modern history. A reporter once asked him "How much money does it take to make a man happy?" Rockefeller held up his index finger, smiled, and replied, "Just one more dollar."

Do we have a chance of getting healthy again? Yes. The **Third Noble Truth** informs us that there is a way to cease the suffering/desire and reach nirvana, the unconditioned state of liberation from suffering. Nirvana is not a place. It is not a Buddhist heaven. Nirvana is not nothingness or annihilation nor is it an eternal state. It is beyond nothing and everything. When strong desires are extinguished, we reach a state of balance because we are no longer suffering. We see the world clearly without the imperfections caused by desire.

What medicine can be prescribed for us to cure our suffering? The **Fourth Noble Truth** sets forth the Noble Eightfold Path, a road map, of sorts, that leads to the elimination of suffering. This set of deceptively simple guidelines, if followed, will help us cleanse ourselves of our constant desires that keep us locked in samsara, the ceaseless cycle of birth-death-rebirth, because we stubbornly cling to desires and attachments that keep us chained to this existence. The Noble Eightfold Path will help us shed the fetters of desire, thus ensuring a more desirable rebirth and, possibly, enlightenment in this lifetime.

Appendix 4

The Noble Eightfold Path

The Buddha discovered that the way to end dukkha was to follow the Middle Way. The temptation to distill the Buddha's teachings into a pithy sentence: "If we just avoid any type of extreme desire or behavior, we'll reach nirvana" must be avoided. The Buddha knew that achieving the Middle Way is far from simple or easy. But to implement the Fourth Noble Truth and help us stay on the road to enlightenment, the Buddha developed the Noble Eightfold Path; which is the Middle Way conveniently divided into distinct steps covering wisdom (steps 1 and 2); morality (steps 3, 4, and 5); and mental discipline (steps 6, 7, and 8).

There is no order or priority for the steps. Each step should be worked on each day. It helps to visualize each step as a spoke in a wheel. For the dharma wheel to roll smoothly, each spoke must be there. The term "right," when used in front of a step, means correct, when based on Buddhist principles. "What Would the Buddha Do" is one way to translate "right" in the Noble Eightfold Path.

<u>Wisdom</u>
1. **Right Understanding**. See things as they really are. Use meditation to stay in the moment without rushing to judgement about the moment.

2. **Right Thought**. Approach situations with kindness toward all sentient beings. Recognize when the ego is driving thoughts and eliminate ego.

Morality
3. **Right Speech**. Think before you speak. Don't let your mouth get ahead of your brain. Don't use abusive language or lie or slander or gossip.
4. **Right Action**. Do nothing that will harm others or that will create ill-will. Obvious examples: don't murder, steal, or engage in sexual misconduct.
5. **Right Livelihood**. Your job should help other people; not hurt them. Professions to avoid include prostitution, drug dealer, and executioner, among others.

Mental Discipline

6. **Right Effort**. Use the correct amount of effort to accomplish tasks. Don't be lazy but don't be a workaholic. Keep your emotions in check.
7. **Right Mindfulness**. All we have is now, this moment; so, we must be mindful of our actions. We live now and the future is not guaranteed. Fixating on past events and/or projecting ahead to what might happen are pointless mental exercises. Now occurs only once; for a split-second. And then it decays. *Now* is the perfect embodiment of the Buddha's teachings; because now dramatically emphasizes that we live only in this current moment: now; and since now is impermanent, it follows that we are also impermanent.
8. **Right Concentration**. Leads to right mindfulness. Focus on awareness of now by concentrating on mindfulness.

Glossary

<u>The first spelling is Sanskrit; the second Pali</u>

Amrapali/Ambapali. A courtesan in Vaisali who invited the Buddha to a meal and gave him a mango grove and land.

Anuttara-Samyak-Sambodhi. All Buddhas have the same attributes: equal, complete, correct, and highest universal knowledge/awareness. <u>Anuttara</u> = supreme, highest, incomparable, unsurpassed, peerless; <u>Samyak</u> = right, correct, true, accurate, complete, perfect, same, identical; <u>Sambodhi</u> = wisdom/perfect wisdom, enlightenment. Thus, all Buddhas have <u>supreme perfect wisdom</u>.[411]

Aniruddha/Anuruddha. Ananda's cousin/half-brother. They were ordained at the same time. Anuruddha became an arhat and was present at the Buddha's parinirvanization. Anuruddha counseled Ananda and the other grieving, unenlightened monks.

Arhat (Arahant). Translated as "A Worthy One." In the Theravada School of Buddhism, monks seek enlightenment only for themselves. An arhat (saint) has gained true insight into the nature of existence. It is the highest level a Theravada monk can reach. The arhat achieves full extinction at parinirvana. "An Arahant had extinguished the fires of craving, hatred, and ignorance, but he still had a residue of fuel as long as he lived in the body, used his senses and mind, and experienced emotions. There was a potential for a further conflagration. But when an Arahant died, these khandha could never be ignited again, and could not feed the flame of a new existence. The Arahant was, therefore, free from samsara and could be absorbed wholly into the peace and immunity of Nibbana"[412] The equivalent level in Mahayana Buddhism is bodhisattva. An arhat and a bodhisattva reach enlightenment with the help of a teacher. A Buddha achieves enlightenment with no help.

Artifacts (aka ***relics***). Bones and ashes of a cremated enlightened person. Includes statues. After the Buddha's body was cremated, the Mallas and other clans fought over who would get the Buddha's relics. The warring clans finally agreed to divide the Buddha's remains among royal families and his disciples. Several centuries later, King Ashoka had 84,000 stupas constructed to hold the relics. In 2017, archeologists discovered human remains, along with Buddhist statues, in a small Chinese village. The inscription on one of the chests indicated that the relics were "the Buddha's teeth and bones" and "were buried in the Mañjuśrī Hall of this temple, on June 22, 1013." The archaeologists did not speculate on whether any of the remains are from the Buddha. The Chinese have claimed that previous discoveries of human remains, including a skull, were the Buddha's; but there's no way to verify the claims.[413]

Asking a Question Three Times. or performing a behavior three times was an Axial Age custom and symbolized the last word or permanence. It appears to be a cultural norm related to interpersonal communication that was prevalent in Buddhist, Christian, and Jewish populations. "According to Jewish law, once something is done three times it is considered a permanent thing, a chazakah.[414] The connection to Buddhism is unmistakable. Right Speech is one of the steps in the Buddhist Noble Eightfold Path. Unnecessary talking or babbling is discouraged; so, knowing that you must ask the Buddha or anyone a question three times forces you to analyze whether the question is really that important. The popular phrase three times is the charm probably had its origin in this ancient social custom.

Ashadha (Sanskrit). The months of June and July on the Buddhist calendar.

Asubha. Translated as 'impurity.' An advanced meditation for those who are lustful or fascinated with the sensual world. Asubha techniques emphasize the less attractive aspects of the world to create dispassion and provide balance. For example, obsession with sex or eating or death or anything is harmful. But contemplation on these events leads to dispassion as we realize everything is temporary and eventually comes to an end. The Buddha successfully used Asubha principles to free Matangi from her sexual obsession with Ananda. Asubha is an advanced meditation technique and should not be attempted by novice meditators.

Axial Age. A period that lasted from about the eighth to the third century BCE. German philosopher Karl Jaspers used the term axial because he believed the period was "pivotal" in the history of mankind. Jaspers noted that new ways of thinking were being independently developed by different cultures during the same historical time frame. These new religions and philosophies changed civilization. In India: Buddhism, Hinduism, Jainism, the Upanisads; China: Daoism, Confucianism; Iran: Zoroastrianism; Palestine: Isaiah, Elijah, Jeremiah; Greece: Homer, Hippocrates, Galen, Virgil, Plato, Socrates, Heraclitus. Although these were radically different cultures and apparently had not been influenced by cross-fertilization of ideas, all developed similar new ways of thinking.

Bhagavan. A term for deity in Jainism and Hinduism, but, since Siddhartha Gautama did not claim to be a deity, Bhagavan is a title of respect for the Buddha. Includes Lord Buddha, The Blessed One, Bhagavan Shakyamuni, or Bhagavan Buddha.

Bhandagama. On his final journey, the Buddha and Ananda stopped by Bhandagama, a Vajjian village near Vesali; and the Buddha gave a discourse to the monks on conditions that lead to nirvana: righteousness, earnest thought, wisdom, and freedom.

Bhikshu. A fully ordained male Buddhist monk. Bhikshus were expected only to meditate and present the Dharma. They were not allowed to work. They moved through successive degrees of postulant, novice, monk, arhat (saint) in the Theravada school or bodhisattva "Buddha candidate" in the Mahayana sect.

Bhikshuni. A fully ordained female Buddhist nun. Bhikshunis were strictly regulated and were totally subservient to Bhikshus, no matter how senior the Bhikshuni or junior the Bhikshu.

Bodhi Tree (Tree of Awakening). A large, ancient pipal tree, considered to be the holiest tree in Buddhism and a direct descendant of the Bodhi Tree under which Siddhartha Gotama was enlightened and became the Buddha. It is located at the Mahabodhi Temple, Bodh Gaya, Bihar, India. A relative of the Bodhi Tree also grows in Jetavana monastery, near present-day Uttar Pradesh, India. The Buddha instructed Ananda to get a sapling from the Bodhi Tree in Bodh Gaya and plant it at the Jetavana monastery, where the sangha was based. The Buddha thought that while he was traveling and teaching the Dharma, pilgrims who came to Jetavana to see him could venerate the tree instead as though he were there. A different, more complicated version, with the same basic plotline, has Ananda apparently delegating getting the sapling to Moggallana, who chose not to just cut a small portion of the Bodhi Tree and replant it. Instead, Moggallana riveted his gaze on the tree in Bodh Gaya and, as a fruit dropped, he scrambled to catch it before it hit the ground. Moggallana gave the fruit to Anathapindika, who, in an elaborate ceremony, planted it in a jar. Miraculously, a sapling, fifty cubits high (almost seventy-four feet) immediately sprung up. The Buddha consecrated this precocious young tree by spending one night under it, in deep meditation. The Anandabodhi Tree, named after Ananda, because the operation was under his direction, is considered the second-holiest tree of Buddhism. Descendants of the original Bodhi

Tree are still alive, two thousand five hundred years after they were originally planted. Two trees are in India and in one in Sri Lanka.

Bodhisattva. "Enlightenment-bound being." Considered the ideal enlightened person by the Mahayana branch of Buddhism. Since all beings are inseparable (non-duality), one should seek enlightenment for everyone, not just oneself, as in Theravada Buddhism. Although enlightened, a bodhisattva chooses to delay entering paradise (nirvana) until all sentient beings achieve enlightenment. The equivalent level in Theravada Buddhism is arhat.

Brahmadanda. Punishment for serious infractions of the Vinaya in which the offending monk is separated, excommunicated, dissociated, and ostracized by the other Bhiksus in the sangha.

Brahmin. A member of the priestly caste in India. The intellectual and spiritual leaders of Indian society. Brahmins were the administrators of India's ancient hymns, rituals, and deities. Although priests were at the top of the social order in India, the caste from which Brahmins were chosen was composed of farmers, warriors, traders, and other professions. Brahmin is not to be confused with *Brahma*, the Hindu God or Brahman, the immortal, eternal truth in Hindu philosophy.

Buddha, The. Translated as "awakened one." A Buddha is described as having supreme enlightenment. A Buddha appears once every 320,000 years to restore the dharma after it's been lost in a period of "dark ages." The current Buddha is Shakyamuni Siddhartha Gautama, born in 563 BCE. A Buddha ranks above an arhat (Theravada) and a bodhisattva (Mayahana) because a Buddha reaches enlightenment without the help of a teacher. Other names for Buddha are Bhagava; the Blessed One; the Master; Shakyamuni; Tagathata; Lokanatha.

Buddha-dharma. Asian term for the "religion of the awakened one." Another name for Buddhism in western languages.

Buddaghosa. A fifth-century Indian commentator and scholar of Theravadin Buddhism. His name means "Voice of the Buddha" in Pali. He Wrote <u>Visuddhimagga</u> (Path of Purification). Buddaghosa is generally considered to be the most influential commentator of Theravadin scriptures.

Buddha-nature. Buddhism teaches that all sentient beings can become a Buddha. Every sentient being, no matter how evil, possesses at least a small amount of love and kindness for another being or, perhaps, only for themselves. If this Buddha nature is identified and tapped into, any sentient being, every sentient being, can become enlightened and a Buddha.

Buddha's Discourses, Accuracy of. It appears that immediately after the Buddha's parinirvanization, his discourses were already being distorted. Ananda, the person who assiduously memorized most of the Buddha's sermons, was disturbed by glaring errors spoken by a young monk. If there were mistakes when the discourses were still fresh on the minds of the disciples, and it was a least a hundred and fifty years before the Sutras were written down, how can we evaluate the accuracy of the Sutras we read today…two thousand five hundred years after the Buddha uttered them? To determine accuracy and reliability, descriptions of an event or interaction can be analyzed for internal consistency. Then, a deduction, based on scholarly research and logic, might be the only way modern readers can assess the validity of discourses purported to be spoken by the Buddha and memorized by Ananda. For example, the assertion that Ananda and the Buddha were the same age does not coordinate with other historical facts indicating that Ananda and Rahula were the same age. Also, the Buddha rejected other job seekers to be his attendant because he thought they were too old. And Ananda lived many years after the Buddha's parinirvanization. These factors, and others, validate the supposition that Ananda was much younger than the Buddha. Comparing various accounts is a reliable method to determine authenticity.

Bullock Cart/Ox Cart. A simple two-wheeled or four-wheeled vehicle pulled by an ox team. One or two passengers sit in front with supplies loaded into the back.

Caṇḍāla. The lowest caste of people in India. A Candali is an outcast, an untouchable.

Canker. karmic predilections and/or karmic propensities. Impediments or fetters or kleshas that delay enlightenment; specifically, the mental defilements of sensual pleasures, craving for existence, and ignorance that result in samsara.

Caste System. Buddhism did not follow the Hindu tradition in ancient India of classifying people into five strict castes or classes. At the top were the Brahmins (priests and scholars); then Kshatryias (kings and warriors); followed by Vaishyas (artisans, merchants, and landowners; Sudras (commoners, peasants, servants, laboring classes/unskilled workers). The Untouchable languished at the bottom of the social structure. These out of caste groups (outcast in English) included tribal people, latrine cleaners, street sweepers, etc. They had the worst jobs imaginable. A man born into a lower caste had no realistic chance of moving up to a higher caste during his/her lifetime. Hard work didn't matter. Intelligence didn't matter. You stayed in the caste you were born in. The only hope for Sudras or Untouchables was to accumulate good karma in this life that might allow a propitious rebirth. The Buddha rejected this unchangeable social stratification and allowed men, and later women, from any caste, to join the sangha and obtain enlightenment. This must have been a strong incentive for middle-and-lower-class Indians who desired upward mobility to join the sangha. The Buddha also assigned seniority to monks based on the date they joined. It meant that a man who was born an untouchable, but joined the sangha a week before a Brahmin, would have seniority over the Brahmin. A woman, however, was considered inferior at birth. If she was lucky enough to be born into an upper-class family, her life was better, and she could perhaps marry a higher-caste man. Lower-caste women had no rights and basically no hope, except for the chance that she could be born a man in the next life. Women were thus forced to be very circumspect and careful in their interactions with men. A higher-caste person could easily interpret those actions as deceitful or manipulative, when it was the only way the lower-caste person could operate in such a prejudiced, caste-bound society. The Buddha's admission of women to the sangha was a huge leap forward in women's rights during that period.

Chandaka (Channa). Siddhartha's groom/charioteer and one of seven co-natals that were born at the same moment as the Buddha. While Chandaka was driving the prince through the streets of Kapilavatthu Siddhartha saw an old man, a sick person, and a corpse. When he saw a holy man, he realized that was the life he wanted. Chandaka helped Siddhartha escape from the palace. In the forest, Siddhartha cut his hair, took off his royal raiment, and gave it to Chandaka to take back to the palace. Chandaka did not want to leave. He wanted to protect Siddhartha from wild beasts and criminals and even expressed an interest in becoming a monk. He also might have been worried about explaining to the King how he helped Siddhartha escape. But he followed Siddhartha's orders and returned to the palace. Channa later became a Buddhist monk and joined the sangha. He used his history with the Buddha to intimidate and criticize other monks, including the Buddha's two chief disciples, Sariputra and Moggallana. The Buddha was unsuccessful in counseling Channa and shortly before his parinirvanization, he told Ananda to impose the brahmadanda punishment on Channa; in which the other monks were told to ghost Channa. They were to ignore him, not speak to him, or advise him, or instruct him until he repented. When he learned of the decree, Channa felt remorse, admitted his wrong deeds, and received a pardon, but not before he fainted three times. Channa eventually became an arahant.

Charnel Grounds. In areas of India and Tibet, where tillable soil to grow food and wood for heat are scarce and valuable, corpses were left uncovered and above-ground to decay. These charnel grounds also served an important religious function in Buddhism by emphasizing the impermanence of life. Monks and ascetics often meditated in charnel grounds.

Chazakah. Hebrew word meaning "take possession." In Jewish law, if something is said three times, it establishes burden of proof.

Co-Natals. Seven beings or things that were born at the exact same moment as the Buddha. The list includes "his future wife Yasodhara; his future groom Chandaka; his future companion Udayin; his future royal elephant; his future great horse Kanthaka; the Bodhi Tree; and four treasure urns"[415] These people and things were destined to play a major role in the Buddha's life.

Councils. Buddhists have convened meetings and councils to ensure that the Buddha's discourses (Sutras) and the monastic rules (Vinaya) are accurate. The **First Council** met shortly after the Buddha's parinirvanization, around 400 BCE to revise, correct, and codify the Buddha's Sutras and to settle issues concerning Vinaya. Ananda recited the Sutas and Upali recited the Vinaya. The **Second Council** addressed primarily Vinaya concerns and was held around 380 BCE, seventy years after the Buddha's parinirvanization. The **Third Council** reportedly occurred in 250 BCE, under the patronage of Emperor Ashoka, but some historians question this date because the meeting is not mentioned in Ashoka's records. The council's stated purpose was to purify the Order by expelling monks who had joined only to gain favor with the King. The **Fourth Council** was early in the first century BCE. The Theravada School and the Sarvastivada School, which later became Mayahana, met separately and discussed the turmoil and violence that occurred after the Order was split. The **Fifth Council** met in Burma in 1871 to recite the Buddha's Sutras and to carefully examine them for consistency. The **Sixth Council** was in 1954, also in Burma. The meeting's objective was to affirm and preserve the genuine Dhamma and Vinaya.

Courtesan. A high-priced call-girl, escort, mistress, harlot, or prostitute serving wealthy, influential, and powerful clients.

Cubit. Ancient method of measuring in which a cubit equals approximately 1.47638 feet.

Dalai Lama. Spiritual leader of the Gelug or "Yellow Hat" school of Tibetan Buddhism. The first Dalai Lama in 1391 and each successive Dalai Lama are reincarnations of Avalokitesvara, the bodhisattva of compassion. The fourteenth and current Dalai Lama is Tenzin Gyatso, born in Tibet, July 6, 1935. In 1959, a Tibetan uprising against the People's Republic of China failed and the fourteenth Dalai Lama fled to India, where he now lives in exile.

Dependent Origination aka **Dependent Arising.** Buddhism does not have a Supreme Being who created the world and created us and who punishes us with boils and plagues of locusts when he's in a bad mood. So, how do things happen in Buddhist cosmology? Buddhism explains that every phenomenon is dependent upon a preceding cause, which leads to other phenomena, and so on. Nothing is self-creating. Everything in the material world depends upon what came before it. We are connected to everyone and everything. This is a deceptively simple concept. One of the few times Ananda was ever criticized by the Buddha was when Ananda declared that he totally understood dependent arising. See duality for additional explanations of causality and connectedness.

Devadada. Ananda's brother was also a monk, and a constant source of irritation and danger to the Buddha. Devadatta unsuccessfully tried to murder the Buddha twice; by starting a rockslide and by releasing a wild, drunken elephant to trample the Buddha. Devadatta routinely fomented discord in the sangha. He once insisted, apparently without thinking it through, that monks should be required to consume only vegetarian food. The Buddha calmly explained that, since monks had to go from door-to-door and beg for their meal, it would be unwise and, basically, rude, to insist on a vegetarian menu from the householders. Monks had to take what they were given and be thankful for it. Devadatta also made several vain attempts to take over the Buddha's ministry. At one point, he claimed that the Buddha was old and tired, suggesting that the Buddha allow him to manage the sangha. Toward the end of his life, suffering from a guilty conscience, Devadatta reportedly was going to ask the Buddha to forgive his earlier actions; but Devadatta never got the chance. As he was walking to the Buddha's monastery, his karma caught up with him. The earth swallowed him up and he was reborn in Avici Hell. Devadatta is an interesting character. He is the antagonist, the Professor Moriarty, to the Buddha's protagonist role and the opposite of the kind and loyal Ananda.

Dharma. The teachings of the Buddha.

Dhyana/jhana. Concentration or meditation.

Duality. Our attempts to separate ourselves from other humans and other sentient beings. We believe we're dualistic, which is just a fancy word that means we believe we are unique, that we each have a separate soul. "I am me and you are you. And I am unique because I am different than you." This dualism inevitably leads to "I am better than you" and "You don't deserve to live here with me" and, eventually, "You don't deserve to live at all." But Buddhist philosophy realizes that we are not separate, independent entities. It's important to remember that duality does not mean that nothing exists; only that nothing exists on its own with a unique, individual essence. We're all part of a huge, living organism. When we hurt another person, we're hurting ourselves, because we're all connected. The Beatles expressed this concept in *I Am the Walrus:* "I am he, as you are he, as you are me, and we are all together."

If we cling to our dualistic beliefs that we each are separate and distinct with a separate and distinct soul, the obvious question is: Where does the soul reside? A popular Buddhist analogy explains it well: "Who is Jane Doe? Where can I find her soul---the one part that makes Jane Doe special? Is Jane Doe her heart or her finger? If I cut off her finger, is she still Jane Doe? If I cut her hair, is she still Jane Doe?" Buddhists answer that we are <u>not</u> unique creations; because if we continue to whittle Jane Doe even down to her atoms, we'll find that there is no central core, no individual soul, because everything is a combination of everything. The popular term, "we are stardust" is factually true. We are composed of everything that has ever existed. And when we die, we will become part of the mix again and will be reborn and the cycle continues unless we reach enlightenment. Did the Buddha discover Quantum Mechanics two thousand five hundred years ago?

Dukkha. The First Noble Truth: Life is Dukkha (translated as suffering.) The uneasiness we feel because our life is disjointed---out-of-balance---like the damaged shopping cart at the grocery store that wobbles and squeaks and is difficult to steer in a straight line.

Emptiness (Sunyata). This term can be confusing to those who do not understand Buddhist doctrines. Emptiness does not mean nihilism or a total void or nothingness. Emptiness is the result of purging ourselves of any defilements, attachments, desires, and in particular, duality. Emptiness occurs when we have scoured our mind so thoroughly of defilements, that we're down to its original, clear, undiluted, pure, unchanging, inherent nature. We are empty of all kleshas, not empty of everything.

Enlightenment. The goal of Buddhism. Reaching nirvana by eliminating the desires that hold us in samsara. In early Buddhism, disciples on the Noble Eightfold Path completed four stages or levels of realization before reaching enlightenment.

Five Precepts. Buddhist ethical guidelines that laypeople on the Noble Eightfold Path must agree to follow. Adherents must abstain from killing, stealing, improper sexual behavior, lying, and intoxicants that cause indolence or dullness of the mind.

Four Places Every Buddhist Should Visit. As the Buddha was becoming parinirvanized, he told Ananda that there are four places in the world worthy of veneration, which would inspire a faithful follower: (1) the birthplace of the Buddha (Lumbini), (2) the place of the Buddha's Enlightenment (Buddha Gaya), (3) the place where the Buddha taught the Dhamma for the first time (Sarnath), and (4) the place of the Buddha's parinirvanization (Kusinara). Anyone who passes away with confident heart while on pilgrimage to these shrines will attain a heavenly rebirth. These four locations are still visited each year by Buddhist pilgrims.

Four Sights (The). Siddhartha Gotama's father tried to shield the young Prince from negative situations that might make him sad. Siddhartha's charioteer, Chandaka, was ordered to take him only to pleasant places. But when Chandaka traveled off the prescribed routes, Siddhartha saw an old man, a sick man, a corpse, and, finally, a holy man. The first three sightings disgusted and confused Siddhartha. However, when he saw the serenity and calmness of the monk, Siddhartha vowed to renounce the worldly life and seek enlightenment,

Ganda-kuti. The name of the Buddha's apartment at the Jetavana monastery, but it is also used to describe his chambers at various other monasteries.

Gautama/Gotama. The Buddha's family name: Siddhartha Gautama.

Householder (Layman in English). An adult male, not a monk, who had a home, spouse, and children. Even if he practiced Buddhist principles faithfully, the householder could not seek enlightenment unless he gave up those three serious attachments and joined a monastery. The Buddha knew this was an unrealistic expectation, so he developed the Five Precepts and other guidelines for laymen. The Buddha said the householder who lived a spiritually meaningful life now would accumulate good karma and would be more likely to have a favorable rebirth as a human. Then, he could join a Buddhist monastery and strive full-time for enlightenment. The two major Buddhism schools differ significantly in their approach to householders. The conservative Theravada School continued the Buddha's policy that only monks could be enlightened. The more inclusive Mahayana School declared that householders had the same opportunity for enlightenment as monks.

Jetavana monastery. Located in present-day Uttar Pradesh, India, the Buddha gave most of his teachings and discourses at this site. The monastery was donated to the Buddha by his chief patron, Anathapindika. The Buddha directed Ananda to plant a Bodhi tree at the monastery for worshipers to venerate in case the Buddha was on-the-road teaching. It was named the Anandabodhi in Ananda's honor. A tree is still there, but it is unlikely to be the original one from two thousand five hundred years ago. The Buddha's hut at the monastery, the Gandhakuti, is still open for visitations.

Kalpa. In Buddhism, the very long period, ranging from 16 million years to 1.3 trillion years, between the creation and recreation of a world or universe.

Kanthaka. Siddhartha's horse and one of the seven beings and things (co-natals) born at the same moment as Siddhartha. The prince rides Kanthaka in his escape from the palace. In one version of the story, when Siddhartha is in the woods taking off his princely attire, Kanthaka does not want to leave the prince and dies immediately of grief. In another version, Kanthaka returns to the palace with Chandaka, but dies of a broken heart a week later.

Kapalivastu. Siddhartha's Gautama's birthplace and the capital city of the Sakya clan, which was ruled by his father, King Suddhodana. Two present-day cities hold possibilities of being the ancient Kapalivastu.

Tilaurakot is in southern Nepal, west of Lumbini Grove, traditionally considered the birthplace of Siddhartha Gautama. Piprahwa, in the Indian state of Uttar Pradesh, is twelve miles from Lumbini. Archaeologists believe a large stupa in Piprahwa could have held portions of the Buddha's ashes that were given to the Sakyan clan. The ruins of several monsasteries nearby also favor Piprahwa as the ancient site of Kapalivastu.

Karma. The residual effects of past actions. The law of cause and effect. We desire, then we act, and some effect, either positive or negative, always results. That effect is karma. People might forgive and forget, but forgiveness is not karma's job and karma never forgets. Every, single, action we do in this life or that we did in previous lives produces either positive karma or negative karma. These karmic bits can ripen, come to fruition, and manifest themselves at any time. You can never escape the effects and the consequences of your actions. Karma will always come back to pay back, either positively or negatively, in this life or a future life. Ripening karma is evident in our daily lives if we are aware. What we commonly call good luck or bad luck is probably karma returning to remind you of your past actions. For example, the good fortune or problems you're having now with your finances or job, or personal relationships might be the result of returning karmic bits that you accumulated through your actions earlier today or hundreds or thousands of lifetimes ago.

When we die, any un-ripened karmic bits just roll over and join the existing karma. The accumulation of positive actions in this life and previous lives could result in a favorable rebirth as a deva, asura, or human. Negative actions, of course, deposit negative karma in the karma bank and can offset the positive karma. Then, an unfavorable rebirth as an animal, hungry ghost, or hell being is possible.

This human form we now inhabit is our best bet to end samsara and rebirth, favorable or unfavorable, forever. If we study Buddhist philosophy, the Four Noble Truths, and conscientiously live and practice the Noble Eightfold Path, it is possible, though very difficult, to achieve nirvana in this lifetime. But even if we're not enlightened in this life, at least we'll be depositing the good stuff into our karma bank for positive future rebirths.

Khandha/Skandhas. Individuals are composed of five aggregates of conditions and functions: a physical body with five senses; feelings ranging from pleasant, unpleasant, or neutral; ideas and concepts; desires and volitions; and self-consciousness. The Buddha has "transformed these five into an expression and embodiment of Dharma."[416] This is a very complicated concept requiring intense study.

Klesha. Desires, strong or conflicting emotions, trouble, passions, or various other defilements that dull the mind and keep us trapped in samsara. The attainment of arhathood extinguishes all kleshes.

Lifespans in the Axial Age. The average lifespan two thousand five hundred years ago was thirty to thirty-five due primarily to the extremely high infant mortality rate. If you survived birth and somehow lived to be an adult, death could still make an unexpected visit. Disease and infectious diseases were rampant. There were no medicines, no antibiotics, no understanding of germs, no understanding of hygiene, no refrigeration of meats. If you became ill, herbal remedies were sometimes used, but, realistically, you just had to let the condition run its course and hope you survived. Other perils, including accidents and murder, were always lurking in the shadows. Of course, a person did not automatically die at the age of thirty. Longevity then, as today, was affected by diet, genetics, overall health, environmental factors, random occurrences, and luck...or karma. The Buddhist doctrine of impermanence has heightened salience when existence is examined. It is obvious that just staying alive---in any historical period---is tentative and by no means guaranteed. Anything can happen at any time. Being trampled by a wild boar was just as unpredictable then as being killed in an automobile crash today.

In 1347, the Black Plague (bubonic plague) spread throughout Asia and Europe, killing one-third of the world's population in three years. The plague returned in 1665 to kill millions more in Europe. In the nineteenth century, during the U.S. Civil War, there was no understanding in the medical community of the importance of cleanliness in preventing infection. And there were no antibiotics. If a soldier was shot in the arm or leg, surgeons amputated the limb. Chloroform and morphine, if the surgeons had it, helped dull the pain. If he was shot in the gut or head, he died. It was as simple as that.

Even into the twentieth century, medical care was still very primitive. The Spanish flu in 1918 infected an estimated 500 million people---one-third of the world's population. Twenty million to 50 million died from the flu, including an estimated six hundred seventy-five thousand Americans. Even as World War I raged across Europe, more U.S. soldiers died from the 1918 Spanish flu pandemic than were killed in combat

The middle to late 20th century brought AIDS and Eboli. Then, in 2020, the COVID pandemic killed more than six hundred seventy thousand Americans with a world-wide death toll of over 4.6 million. After a brilliant world-wide effort, scientists quickly developed effective vaccines.

In 1983, friends celebrated blues/ragtime pioneer Eubie Blake's one hundredth birthday, although he was really ninety-six. Blake purportedly said: "If I had known I was going to live this long, I'd have taken better care of myself!" So, perhaps the Buddha lived to be eighty and Ananda lived to one hundred twenty because they took good care of themselves. Living to an advanced age was certainly unusual for that time; but it is just as noteworthy today.

Lokanatha. Translated as protector of the world or lord of the world. Another name for the Buddha.

Mahayana. A major Buddhist sect translated as "great" (*Maha*) "raft" (*yana*). Mahayana can be described as Buddhism for the masses. It was the largest and more inclusive than Theravadans because Mahayanans allowed laymen or householders to seek nirvana. The Dalai Lama belongs to the Mahayana sect.

Maitreya (S) Metteyya (P). Sanskrit for friendship. In the future, the dharma will be forgotten on Earth and a bodhisattva named Maitreya will appear. He will achieve enlightenment and teach the dharma. Maitreya is currently residing in Tusita Heaven and is the successor to the current Gautama Buddha.

Malla. A powerful clan that ruled territory in eastern India during the Buddha's lifetime. Pava, where the Buddha ate his last meal and Kusinara, where the Buddha became parinirvanized, were under Malla rule.

Mara. The Evil One, The Tempter, The Lord of Death. The Buddhist version of Satan or the Devil. As Siddhartha Gautama was nearing enlightenment under the Bodhi tree, Mara tried to break his concentration by sending three demons disguised as beautiful women to tempt him, but Siddhartha was unmoved. Then Mara attacked with hurricanes, torrential rains, and showers of flaming rocks, but the unperturbed Siddhartha sat quietly as the molten rocks turned to flower petals and fell harmlessly at his feet. In a final, desperate attempt to undermine Siddhartha's confidence, Mara demanded that Siddhartha produce a witness to testify that he deserved to succeed in gaining enlightenment where others had failed. Siddhartha had practiced the virtues leading to enlightenment over countless lifetimes and meditated under countless Bodhi trees, so he silently extended his right hand and gently touched the ground. Earth responded with a thunderous roar: "I bear witness!" Mara was soundly defeated and went slinking away, demoralized. Siddhartha Gotama soon became the Buddha.

Satan's temptation of Jesus is very similar. Since the Buddha lived 500 years before Jesus, it is convenient to assume that the writers of the New Testament were inspired by the Buddha's tribulations. However, it is not clear whether there was significant cross-pollination between the two religions that gave early Christians access to Buddhist writings. Perhaps overcoming temptation is simply a universal theme that all men on a path to greatness must conquer. Today, some consider Mara and Satan as merely metaphors for a person's ego run amok.

Marks or Signs of a Great Man. These marks must be present on the body of a Buddha. The holy-man Asita inspected the new-born Siddhartha Gautama and discovered the Signs of a Great Man. This Indian tradition dates to Brahmanism and was based on cultural perceptions of physical beauty. Historians of the time often describe the Buddha using terms such as "glowing, golden skin," "lotus-blue eyes," "evenly-spaced, very white teeth," "and, apparently, a requirement for a Buddha, "a nice smile." There are, however, some weird attributes: immense torso; large, long tongue; oxen eyelashes, elongated skull, and projecting heels. Ananda missed being a Buddha by only one mark. One wonders which of the 32 marks Ananda did not have.

- He has feet with a level sole so that he places his foot evenly on the ground and touches the ground evenly with the entire sole.
- He has the mark of a thousand-spoked wheel on the soles of his feet.
- He has projecting heels.
- He has long fingers and toes.
- His hands and feet are soft skinned.
- He has netlike lines on palms and soles.
- He has high raised ankles.
- He has taut calf muscles like an antelope.
- He can touch his knees with the palms of his hands without bending.
- His sexual organs are concealed in a sheath.

- His skin is the color of gold. His body is more beautiful than all the gods.
- His skin is so fine that no dust can attach to it.
- His body hair are separate with one hair per pore.
- His body hair are blue-black, the color of collyrium, and curls clockwise in rings.
- He has an upright stance like that of brahma.
- He has the seven convexities of the flesh. The seven convex surfaces,/ on both hands, both feet, both shoulders, and his trunk.
- He has an immense torso, like that of a lion.
- The furrow between his shoulders is filled in.
- The distance from hand-to-hand and head-to-toe is equal.
- He has a round and smooth neck.
- He has sensitive tastebuds.
- His jaw is like that of lion's.
- He has a nice smile.
- His teeth are evenly spaced.
- His teeth are without gaps in-between.
- His teeth are quite white.
- He has a large, long tongue.
- He has a voice like that of Brahma.
- He has very blue eyes.
- He has eyelashes like an ox.
- He has a white soft wisp of hair in the center of the brow.
- His head is like a royal turban. (an elongated cranium.)[417]

Middle Way. Primary doctrine of Buddhism. Avoid extremes. A life focused only on sensual pleasures is just as destructive as a life focused only on asceticism.

Mirror of Dharma. akin to an owner's manual for Buddhism. It includes pertinent teachings of the Buddha, Buddhist rituals, and advice on how to rid oneself of desires that hinder the quest for enlightenment. The Buddha explained its purpose: "What, O Ananda, is the Mirror of the Dharma? Herein a noble disciple has absolute confidence in the Buddha, Dharma and Sangha. Because of his confidence, he spends much time to reflect or think about the great qualities of the Triple Gem. These reflections will help him develop the great qualities within himself and the power to concentrate the mind. These results will help him attain the first stage of sainthood (Sotapanna). Possessing this Mirror of Dharma, a noble disciple shall be able to predict for himself that he shall not fall back to lower states like hell, the animal world, the ghost world and other sorrowful and unhappy states."[418]

Mount Meru. The center of the Buddhist cosmos, Meru is surrounded by seven concentric circles of mountains, seas, and four continents. Below the Himalayas, in the southern continent, is India. The six realms of existence are on the slopes of Mount Meru.

Nanda. The Buddha's younger half-brother/stepbrother. When Siddhartha's biological mother, Maya, died, his father married Maya's younger sister, Prajapati, who had earlier given birth to a son named Nanda with Siddhartha's father. Some reports indicate that Prajapati "put out her own son to be looked after by a nurse and brought up Siddhartha as her own, with all the love of a real mother."[419] Eight years after Siddhartha left home in his search for enlightenment, he became the Buddha and returned to his hometown. He ordained many of his male relatives into the sangha. Concurrently, Prince Nanda was preparing to marry a beautiful princess. The Buddha felt the sangha was a better choice for his stepbrother and he was such an intense, persuasive speaker, that he convinced Nanda to abandon his wife-to-be on their wedding day to join the sangha. To seal the deal, the Buddha enlisted one of his chief disciples, Upatissa, to ordain Nanda. The emotional high Nanda felt by the Buddha's attention was only temporary. Nanda was soon hit by the cold realization that the ascetic life of the monastery did not hold the same delights as his former luxurious life with the alluring princess he left at the altar. This was a perfect example of the Buddhist philosophy of impermanence. Nanda was extremely unhappy and was not adjusting well to the sangha. He complained a lot and became somewhat of a character in the Order. He lived up to his other name as Sundarananda (handsome Nanda). He showed "a quite unmonastic concern about his appearance, using cosmetics in the manner of fashionable men of the time, and wearing neatly pressed robes. For his begging rounds, he took not an ordinary bowl, but an elegant piece of glazed pottery."[420]The Buddha patiently counseled his frustrated half-brother, who eventually extinguished his attachments to the world; in particular, his sensual longing for his forlorn bride-to-be. With those strong emotional fetters cut, Nanda became an arhat.

Monastic Regulations for Bhikkuni.

1. A Bhikkhuni (nun) should always respect a Bhikkhu (monk), even if the monk is junior to her in the Order.
2. For safety concerns, a nun shall not spend the rainy season in a place where there are no monks.
3. Twice a month, the nuns shall ask the monks the time when the monastic discipline is recited and request for a monk to come to advise and admonish nuns who have deviated from monastic rules.
4. At the termination of the rainy season retreat, the final ceremony shall be held in an assembly of both monks and nuns.
5. Certain offenses committed by nuns should be dealt with by assemblies of both monks and nuns. The assembly of nuns deals with only minor transgressions and some of a personal nature to women.
6. A novice nun shall receive higher ordination after a training period of two years. (Sometimes, monks were given higher ordination immediately after ordination.)
7. A nun should not rebuke a monk under any circumstances.
8. A monk can admonish a nun who has transgressed the monastic discipline.[421]

Naraka (S) Niraya (P). Buddhist hell.

Nirvana. The goal of Buddhism. Defining and understanding nirvana is difficult. We must rely on knowledge and perceptions gained in this impermanent, sensory world, which is filled only with mirages of reality. We are mired in this muddy illusion of life. How can we be expected to define, to understand, to grasp the eternal, the unknowable? Let's give it a shot, anyway.

Although the literal meaning of nirvana is extinction, it is not total annihilation or nihilism, as it is sometimes misinterpreted. Nirvana is the state of existence in which the three fires that feed the finite self---greed, hatred, and delusion---are blown out, extinguished, releasing us from desires and suffering and karma and samsara. Nirvana is a boundless state of freedom, "a condition in which all identification with the historical experience of the finite self disappears, while experience as such not only remains, but is heightened beyond recognition"[422]

The Buddha was often asked the question: What exactly is nirvana? He responded by explaining that our born, originated, made, and conditioned existence keeps us bound in samsara. What we escape to is nirvana, the unborn, unoriginated, unmade, and unconditioned state. That's a rather vague answer; but when the Buddha was asked big questions, such as, "where did we come from and where are we going?" he would often respond with the parable of the poisoned arrow. He was saying, in so many words, "don't worry about that. You'll just waste time and you'll probably be dead before you ever know the answer. Concentrate on improving yourself now."

Along the same lines of clever answers, Nagasena, one of the Buddha's principal followers, answered a monk's question of "what is nirvana" with his own question:

> *Nagasena*: "Is there such a thing as wind?"
> *Monk*: "Yes, revered sir."
> *N*: "Please, sir, show the wind by its color or configuration
> or as thin or thick or long or short."

M: "But it is not possible, revered Nagasena, for the wind to be shown; for the wind cannot be grasped in the hand or touched; yet wind exists."

N: "If, sir, it is not possible for the wind to be shown, well then, there is no wind."

M: "I, revered Nagasena, know there is wind; I am convinced of it, but I am not able to show the wind."

N: "Even so, sir, nirvana exists; but it is not possible to show nirvana"[423]

When we clean our home, it doesn't disappear. When we wash and vacuum our car, it doesn't cease to exist. The home and the car are just clean, down to their essential elements. Likewise, when we attain enlightenment and enter nirvana, we don't explode into nothingness. Enlightenment/nirvana is what remains after we deep clean our minds. Then, we have unlimited horizons. To quote the Who: "I can see for miles and miles."

Our miniature Schnauzer likes to sit on the guest bed, look out the window, and talk to the students as they walk to class. I entered the room one day and the blinds were closed; but Ra'sco was staring intently through a tiny slit in the blinds. I pulled the blinds up to expose the entire window and he reacted immediately to the rush of new, clear perceptions. He had assumed only the small area he could see was all that was possible, the entire world, until I raised the blinds.

In the same way, the enlightened and unenlightened might be interacting with each other in a social situation, but their perceptions are totally different. Like Ra'sco, the unenlightened see the world through a small, hazy, sliver of perception because they must filter every, single, input through the confused jumble of fetters, jealousies, desires, attachments, and anger that fills their mind. But, when enlightenment has destroyed the cankers that bind us to samsara, we are able to experience the world's full beauty. The enlightened have extinguished unhealthy desires and attachments that cloud our vision. What remains is a clear, unimpeded, high-definition view of the world.

Order (The). Another name for the sangha or Buddhism.

Ordination as a Monk. When Buddhism divided into two distinct approaches, the Theravada School continued the Buddha's approach to train its monks. Each level eliminates several of the Ten Fetters that keep us in samara. At <u>level one</u>, as a stream-enterer, a monk has broken the first three fetters (belief in personality, doubt about the path to liberation, and attachment to rules and rituals) and can attain enlightenment within seven lifetimes. The stream-enterer imagery is revealing. The monk enters a course of study and learning. It can be a slow process of floating down a peaceful stream or, for some students, a much quicker, fast-flowing river. It depends on how dedicated and sincere the learner is about facing and cleansing the most common hindrances to enlightenment. <u>Level two</u>, a once-returner, has significantly weakened fetters 4 and 5 (sensuous craving, ill will/aversion) and will be reborn as a human just one more time before reaching stage four. At <u>level three</u>, a nonreturner has eliminated fetters 1 through 5 and will not be reborn as a human. <u>Level four</u> is the highest level. This is the arhat, who has eliminated all ten fetters and achieved enlightenment and nirvana. The arhat will never again experience the suffering of samsara.

Pali Language. The Tipitaka Canon for the Theravada School of Buddhism is written in Pali. The Buddha is believed to have used a dialect of Pali when he spoke. Pali and Sanskrit are similar, but one did not spring from the other. Each developed independently.

Parinirvana. The death of someone who became enlightened during his or her lifetime. Samsara, karma, and all skandas were eliminated when the person was enlightened; so, at death, the enlightened one reaches total extinction.

Parinirvanize/Parinirvanization is used to describe only the Buddha's transition. "Buddhist texts do not usually speak of the Buddha as entering or attaining parinirvana; rather, they describe him as being parinirvanized, which means completely extinguished. The Buddha himself is said to have indicated that it was not fruitful to think about the ontological meaning of nirvana. After death the saint was beyond imagining in terms of either being or non-being."[424]

Pasenadi, King of Kosala. Ruled the kingdom of Kosala. One of his consorts was the daughter of Prince Siddhartha's cousin. Kosala converted to Buddhism early in the Buddha's ministry and heard many of the Buddha's discourses. For example, when Kosala's wife, Queen Mallika, gave birth to a girl (Vajir), the king was very disappointed. Sons were treasured, daughters, not so much. But the Buddha convinced the king that if you think about it, a well-brought-up daughter can be more valuable than a son because you might be able to marry her off to someone rich and powerful. The Buddha urged the king to "bring her up with love and devotion." The king followed the Buddha's advice and later, a propitious marriage resulted in the princess becoming the Queen of Magadha. The Buddha's advice to the king flew in the face of prevailing Indian social attitudes that considered women as inferior to men. This incident is further evidence that the Buddha was not a misogynist. When King Kosala's beloved grandmother died, the Buddha reminded the grieving king that all things are impermanent:

> All beings are mortal, they end with death.
> They have death in prospect.
> All vessels wrought by the potter,
> whether they are baked or unbaked,
> are breakable---they end broken.
> They have breakage in prospect.

King Kosala was also the main character in a parable the Buddha discussed about giving with a free heart. King Kosala saw the generosity of Anathapindika, one of the Buddha's primary benefactors. Perhaps to one-up his rival, King Kosala invited five hundred monks to his palace for their daily meal. The excitement eventually wore off, since all things are impermanent, and the king ordered his servants to distribute lunch to the monks. Later, he discovered the monks were not eating the food, but giving it to their lay followers, who then gave some of it back to the monks. The baffled king asked the Buddha why the monks were doing this. The Buddha replied that the monks were uncomfortable in accepting the donations because the king's servants were rude to the monks, calling them parasites and telling them to work for their meals. Since the food was not given in a sense of generosity, the monks gave the food to the lay devotees, who were overjoyed that they were able to feed the monks. If there is no joy in giving, why should one give?[425]

Poisoned Arrow (Parable of the). The Venerable Malunkyaputta was at Jetta's Grove with the Buddha and the sangha. After a discourse by the Buddha, he was curious about several issues he felt the Buddha had not explained to his satisfaction. He asked the Buddha (1) whether the world is eternal; (2) whether the soul and the body are one and the same thing; and (3) whether after death a Tathagata exists or not. The Buddha replied that he never promised Malunkyaputta that he would answer those questions and he used a parable to explain that such questions were unnecessary and only hindered the quest for enlightenment.

> It is as if, Malunkyaputta, there were a man struck by an arrow that was smeared thickly with poison; his friends and companions, his family and relatives would summon a doctor to see to the arrow. And the man might say, "I will not draw out this arrow so long as I do not know whether the man by whom I was struck was of the Brahman, Ruler, Trader, or Servant class; or so long as I do not know his name or his family; whether he was tall, short, or of medium height; whether he was black, brown, or light-skinned, whether he comes from this or that village, town, or city; whether the bow was a *capa* type or a *kodanda* type, whether the bow string was of the *akka* plant, reed, sinew, hemp, or the milk-leaf tree,

whether the shaft was taken from the wild or cultivated. whether the shaft was fitted with the feathers of a vulture, heron, falcon, peacock, or *sithilahan*u; whether the shaft was bound with the sinews of a cow, buffalo, antelope, or monkey, whether the arrowhead was a barb, a razor-point, a *vekanda* type, iron, a 'calf-tooth', or an 'oleander leaf.' The Buddha concluded, "That person would die and still he would not know this." And, just in case the parable wasn't clear enough, the Buddha said Malunkyaputta's questions were simply a waste of time: "I have not explained. And why have I not explained this? Because it is not relevant to the goal, it is not fundamental to the spiritual life, it does not lead to disenchantment, to dispassion, to cessation, to peace, to direct knowledge, to full awakening, to nibbana. Therefore, I have not explained this,"[426]

The Buddha used this long, complicated parable to show how we can become fixated on unimportant details and fail to see the big picture.

Realms of Existence. Until we reach enlightenment, we must endure a continuous cycle of birth, death, and rebirth (samsara) until we extinguish the desires that keep us bound to this existence; in other words, until we get it right. These reborn souls must go somewhere, and earth can't accommodate all the reborn unenlightened, so Buddhism postulates countless worlds like earth sprinkled through the cosmos. Buddhism and Christianity differ greatly in their perceptions of the afterlife. Christianity requires belief in all-powerful god who decides who will go to heaven or hell. Buddhist cosmology does not recognize a supreme-being. The Buddha stressed that each person's individual actions determine his/her fate. Belief in a specific person or deity is not necessary to reach nirvana. In 1875, English poet William Ernest Henley elegantly interpreted this Buddhist philosophy in Invictus: "I am the master of my fate, I am the captain of my soul."

Christians believe heaven or hell is eternal. Buddhists believe nothing lasts forever. Although the god/demigod realm is impermanent;

luckily, so is Naraka. A million lifetimes in the hottest Naraka would be very unpleasant; but at least it will end eventually.

The Buddhist afterlife is based on karma, translated as action. If we die unenlightened, the karma we have built up through thousands or millions of previous lives determines whether we'll be reborn in a desirable realm as a god, demigod, or human; or in an unfortunate realm as an animal, hungry ghost, or hell-being. Each realm is only a temporary stop-over. The only way to avoid rebirth somewhere is enlightenment.

After an unenlightened person dies, assignment to the appropriate realm occurs automatically, with no interference from a god. We determine, by our actions, where we will end up when we die. The Buddhist afterlife process can be visualized as a huge doctor's waiting room, with millions of deceased unenlightened individuals reading year-old magazines and playing with their cell phones, while the cumulative positive and negative karma from each person's previous lives is fed into the cosmic computer, which clicks and hums while calculating the appropriate afterlife realm and length of stay for each person.

The home-base of the Buddhist world-system, where the deceased unenlightened receive their tickets to their afterlife destinations, is Mount Meru, which rises to the heavens and goes deep into the bowels of earth. Mount Meru is inconceivably massive and houses the seven realms of Buddhist afterlife.[427]

Gods (devas/celestial beings.) Gods have the highest level of samsara and live luxurious lives in palaces with jewels and sensual pleasures. There are six deva heavens, with Tusita as the swankiest. Gods have a lifespan of around 350 human years. The downside of this realm is that gods sometimes mistake it for nirvana, so they do not try to create more good karma. As a result, when they have exhausted the good karma and die, only the negative karma remains, and they are cast into a lower realm.

Demigods (asuras.) They experience some, but not all the pleasures of the God Realm. Asuras are plagued by jealousy and competitiveness.

They constantly fight with the devas, and never win, so they do not enjoy their privileged realm.

Humans. We'll return to the human realm in a moment, but first....

Animals. This is the highest of the three lower realms. Animals must constantly search for food, while they live in fear of being another animal's dinner. The animal realm might be the most unpleasant of the lower realms because mammals, for instance, are sentient beings with limited intelligence. They express feelings. They might recognize their surroundings and their predicament; not enough food, predators trying to eat them, but they can't change anything, because they're controlled by primal survival instincts. They blindly behave with stubborn close-mindedness. We can only hope that the dharma we teach to our pets will somehow, at some level, penetrate their minds and help them achieve a human rebirth. The frustration of these higher-level animals must be intense. The fear in your dog's eyes during a thunderstorm is an example of a sentient, intelligent, feeling being, able to recognize danger at a basic level, but totally unable to analyze it or understand it or do anything about it.

Hungry Ghosts (pretas). Those who lived their lives deluded by greed, lustful desires, and miserliness become wandering, frustrated spirits with a never-ending, constant hunger and thirst that cannot be satisfied. They have huge, protruding, bloated stomachs representing their intense cravings; but their long, skinny necks prevent them from satisfying their overwhelming desires. Pretas generally live underground with a life span of several thousand years, but they can travel back and forth between subterranean and above-ground. Pretas are visible to some humans who have advanced karma. Many humans have the same characteristics as pretas, so they not only suffer their unquenchable desires while on earth, but later in the hungry ghost realm.

Hell-Beings (naraks). Early Buddhists, along with Christians 500 years later, had vivid imaginations when it came to punishment for misdeeds. Murder, rape, and other obviously heinous acts meant a long stay in Naraka, the Buddhist hell. Even intense thoughts that become strong attachments; for example, hatred and anyone who commits one of the cardinal sins or slanders the true law, could also lead to rebirth as a hell-being.

Naraka can be extremely cold or extremely hot. Naraks are imprisoned underground until the ripened karma that brought them to hell is exhausted. Rebirth in one of the eight hot hells can last up to nine billion human years. Although Sanjiva, at level one, is the mildest of the hot hells, inhabitants are pelted with molten lead and cut into pieces. The worst of the hot hells is level eight, Avichi. Here, the condemned are roasted in an enormous blazing oven. The suffering is uninterrupted, incessant, constant.

The eight cold hells are just as gruesome and uncomfortable. Inhabitants of Arbuda, level one of the cold hells, live their lives naked and alone dealing with constant blizzards on a bleak, dark, cold, windy, desolate plain. Those whose karma brought them to Mahapadma, the coldest hell at level eight, "...are crushed within mountains of frozen rock." Their bodies begin to crack and turn blue, then red. "Karmically created insects and small animals come to feed at our open sores, but there is nothing we can do---for we are frozen into immobility."[428] When death mercifully comes to the narak, the person does not necessarily move to a higher realm. If the negative karma has not been exhausted, the narak might be reborn into the same realm or a lower realm and will suffer the tortures of the damned again and again, over and over, until the negative karma finally runs out.

We are reborn into one of the six realms because we desperately cling to worldly desires in a vain effort to make them permanent, which is impossible, so we are snatched back to a physical existence. Everything in this world is a combination of separate atoms, which are all impermanent. The nothing lasts forever concept in Buddhism is comforting to many people. For example, an intense relationship with a person will end someday, one way or another. That prospect might seem distressing, but it doesn't mean that an intense relationship cannot occur again. Although all positive experiences will eventually end, it might be comforting to recognize that negative occurrences are also impermanent. When bad things happen, when everything goes wrong, it will not be bad and sad forever. We can start anew.

Many self-help philosophies use Buddhist principles. For example, the live now movement stresses that everything that happened in the past is just a memory. Tomorrow, or an hour from now, hasn't happened yet and it might not happen, if that meteor on a million-year journey from deep space, falls on your head. All we have is now and now is temporary, it's already gone!

Since impermanence is central to Buddhist belief, it follows that any realm we inhabit after death is also temporary. That sounds good at first, especially if you end up in a lower realm. But there's a catch. It's very difficult to move out of the Animal, Hungry Ghost, or Hell-Being realms because the dharma is not accessible. That's the bad news. The good news is the Christian threat of burning in hell for an eternity is not part of Buddhist theology. Granted, spending millions of rebirths as a Hell-Being might seem like forever, but the bad karma will eventually be exhausted, and the unfortunate sweaty or frozen person might be able to move up to a more comfortable existence. In comparison to a hell-being or a hungry ghost, the animal realm might seem like heaven, unless, of course, you're reborn as a chicken, pig, or steer, in which case you'll more than likely end up on someone's plate for dinner.

And after the animal karma finally burns out, maybe you'll have some good karma from earlier lives that will allow you to be reborn in one of the upper realms for several thousand lifetimes, but even the more desirable realms are only temporary. Inhabitants of the Gods and Demi-Gods realms lived good lives and did not accumulate a lot of negative karma when they were humans, but they are not enlightened, so they are still caught in samsara. Eventually, old negative karma will catch up with them and they'll be thrown out of their cushy *God* or *Demi-God* realm and might end up in a lower place. *Animal, hungry ghost,* and *hell-being* realms are unpleasant, but also only temporary. Which realm is the most desirable? The only one left is the one we now inhabit: the human realm. And there's a very important reason why being human is a big advantage.

Humans. Rebirth as a human is, in Buddhist terms, propitious, since only humans have access to the Buddha's teachings. We should use each moment in this human form wisely; because the <u>Dhammapada</u> (verse 182) notes that "it is hard to obtain human birth, harder to live like a human being, harder still to understand the dharma, but hardest of all to attain nirvana." [429]

In the first noble truth, the Buddha states: Life is suffering. Illness, old age, and death will eventually claim all of us. Extreme wealth, intense workouts, vitamins, daily prayers, meditation, or tithing to the church cannot stop the cycle. And samsara will continue in countless millions, billions of births-deaths-rebirths. The desires and clinging to material things keep us attached to this temporal world. We are trapped in the cycle of birth-death-rebirth, and we suffer and suffer and suffer until we use the razor-sharp scalpel of mindfulness to completely excise, to cut from our minds, those fetters so we can achieve enlightenment.

Samapatti. Translated as acquisition of truth. An advanced Buddhist meditation technique in which the meditator leaves the outward sensory world and concentrates inwardly to perceive the true nature of things. Samapatti can address specific attachments. To free ourselves of lust or sexual attachments, we must see the sexy, beautiful woman as she really is---an impermanent combination of atoms that defecates, urinates, perspires, has wax in her ears, mucous in her nose, and yellow film on her teeth. An extreme fear of death is approached by meditating on death and understanding that everyone will die. Everyone will decompose and become a stinking, rotting corpse. But, as Buddhism postulates, death is also impermanent. Samapatti helps us recognize that freeing ourselves of fetters in this physical world and achieving nirvana is the answer; not suffering another rebirth.

Samsara. The cycle of birth-death-rebirth caused by our desires and attachments to things in this world that are impermanent. The fetters, kleshas, and attachments that we desperately cling to in this finite life in a futile attempt for permanence leave strands that attach us to this world and do not allow us to progress when we die. Through rebirth. the strands pull us back to this existence to finish what we've started. Following the Noble Eightfold Path will stop samsara and thus eliminate suffering because the desires and attachments that keep us bound to samsara will be extinguished.

sangha. (lower case) Translated from Pali as "community." In Buddhism, it includes members accepted into the Order and lay followers.

Sangha. (Upper case) The third of the Three Jewels of Buddhism, with the Buddha and Dharma.

Sanskrit Language. Developed in the Vedic period in India. Sanskrit is older than Pali and was used in early religious writings in Hinduism, Jainism, and Buddhism. The Mahayana School of Buddhism has many writings in Sanskrit.

Sekha. A disciple who has reached one of the lower stages of awakening. A learner or trainee.

Shakyamuni. Silent Sage of the Sakya Clan. Name given to Siddhartha Gautama when he left home and searched for enlightenment.

Sheath-encased penis. One of the thirty-two characteristics of a great man is the ability to draw the penis into the body, preventing lustful thoughts in anyone who sees him naked.

Siddhartha Gautama. The Buddha's birth name. The literal translation is "all is fulfilled."

Silence in Conversations. Silence is an integral component of Buddhism, which teaches natural phenomena are only composites and fundamentally empty of inherent meaning. Therefore, speech and the absence of speech are equally powerful. Right speech, the third step of the Noble Eightfold Path, advises us to avoid babbling and unnecessary talking. Silent meditation, contemplation, and wordless insight are required to achieve enlightenment. The culture and issue at hand must be considered when determining whether silence indicates agreement or disagreement. For example, the Buddha was focused on leading people to enlightenment. He did not waste his time and energy on superfluous chatter. As a master teacher, the Buddha corrected misinterpretations of the Dhamma by monks or laymen but remained silent to indicate agreement if the person correctly understood the principle. In mundane situations, as when Cunda invited the Buddha and his entourage to have lunch, the Buddha's silence was understood by all to be his acceptance.

Sotopanna. A stream-enterer. The lowest of the four stages leading to enlightenment. The person has successfully freed himself from the first three fetters

Srigupta. Belonged to a rival sect and out of jealousy tried to murder the Buddha by poisoning his food and luring him into a pit of fire. The Buddha graciously forgave Srigupta and saved him "from spite and crime and showed how mercy conquers e'en a foe"[430]

Suddhodana. Siddhartha Gautama's father and King of the Sakya clan.

Sutra. Thread. A teaching, discourse, or scripture of the Buddha believed to be in his own words.

Tathagata. "Thus-perfected one." Another name for the Buddha. A person who has achieved supreme enlightenment. The Buddha often used this term when referring to himself or other Buddhas.

Tejokasina. Translated as fire-kasina (meditation). One of ten kasina exercises in which the meditator attempts to settle his/her mind by concentrating fully on an object, such as a rock or a candle or a distant tree, until all sense-activity ceases and one enters the first jhana or Buddhist meditative state.

Ten Fetters. To reach enlightenment, the ten fetters/bonds that bind us to samsara must be broken: belief in personality or individuality;

doubt about the path to liberation; attachment to precepts, vows, rules, rituals; sensuous craving/desire; ill will/aversion; desire for form; desire for formless; conceit/pride; restlessness/agitation; ignorance.[431]

Theravada. Older and more conservative school than Mahayana. Theravada focuses on the individual monk who must reach nirvana through his own efforts and the wisdom he attains by constant study and meditation. Serious seekers must become monks, live in a monastery, and devote their entire lives to the quest for enlightenment. It cannot be a part-time endeavor. The all-inclusive Mahayana sect (the large raft/great raft) dubbed this monks-only group Hinayana (the small raft). The monks-only disciples understandably thought that name was demeaning, so they began to call their sect Theravada, translated as "the tradition of the elders," because they believed their approach more accurately reflected the Buddha's original intention that only monks should seek enlightenment. It is considered an insult to use the term Hinayana to describe members of Theravada.

Three Jewels. Buddhists repeat the following chant three times:

> I take refuge in the Buddha.
> I take refuge in the Dharma.
> I take refuge in the Sangha.
> For a second time…
> For a third time…

The Three Jewels, the Buddha, Dharma, and Sangha, provide Buddhists with emotional comfort in times of stress; but, most importantly, the Three Jewels open the consciousness so meditation can lead to deeper spiritual guidance. Buddhists meditate. Christians pray. Each are seeking help, but Christians must believe in Jesus, an external powerful god, for assistance. Buddhists rely on the Buddha Nature, present within all of us to attain enlightenment without the requirement that we worship a supreme being.

Thus have I heard/Thus I have heard. At the first Buddhist council, around 400 BCE, Ananda recited the Buddha's teachings for the gathering. It was decided that, to make sure discourses attributed to the Buddha were authentic, each Sutra that Ananda heard the Buddha say would begin with "Thus have I heard" or, in some translations, "Thus I have heard."

Tipitaka/Tripitaka. The "three baskets" for organizing Buddhist theology: Sutra (discourses), Vinaya (organization), and Abhidharma (philosophical issues.)

Tusita Heaven. The residence of devas and is one of the highest realms of sensual pleasure that can be reached through meditation. Siddhartha Gautama lived in Tusita heaven before he was. reborn on Earth as the Buddha. Maya, Siddhartha's mother, was in Tusita heaven when she returned to Earth for the Buddha's funeral. Maitreya, the bodhisattva who will later be born as the next Buddha, currently resides there. Time in Tunista is calculated very differently than on Earth.

Tusita	Earth
24 hours	400 years
1 month	12,000 years
1 year	144,000 years

The lifespan of a Tusita deva is 4,000 heavenly years.

Udumbara Tree. Udumbara is Sanskrit meaning "an auspicious flower from heaven." In Buddhist theology, it blossoms only once, every three thousand years, and heralds the coming of the next Buddha. The flower also symbolizes events of rare occurrence. In 1997, Udumbara blossoms were reportedly spotted on a Buddhist statue in a South Korean temple and in 2010, Chinese media reported sightings of the flower. It is unclear of the time frame between sightings of the Udumbara blossoms and the appearance of the new Buddha.[432]

Upsaka (masculine) *Upasika* (feminine). Translated as attendant. Also known as householder. Followers of the Buddha who are not monks, nuns, or novices and who undertake certain vows. Modern connotation is lay devotee or devout lay follower.

Vedic Period/Vedic Age. Early Indian history (fifteen hundred to five hundred BCE.) The Sanskrit language, used in many Buddhist writings, was developed. Specific roles were assigned to each person, based on his/her social class. Women had no rights. Hinduism emerged in the early Vedic Period. Buddhism later incorporated many Vedic and Hindu concepts, such as karma and dharma.

Viceroy. An official who is appointed by a monarch to run a country or province.

Vinaya. Code of conduct; code of discipline for monks and nuns.

Watches. Early civilizations often divided the twenty-four-hour day into specific watches, in which soldiers "stood watch" for a certain period to guard the community. Buddhism adapted the watch tradition and further delineated a day with specific sessions for the Buddha's activities. The times and activities below are approximate and gleaned from various sources.

The Morning Session   **(4.00 a.m. to 12.00 noon)**

The Buddha got up at 4.00 a.m., washed, and meditated for an hour. From 5:00-6:00 a.m., he used his mental eye to look throughout the world to see if anyone needed help. At 6.00 a.m. he put on his robe and helped the needy or went on his begging rounds. He was often accompanied by his monks, who followed behind him in single file.

The Afternoon Session   **(12.00 noon to 6.00 p.m.).**

The Buddha taught the dharma to the monks and answered their questions for two hours. He would then go to his room and again use his mental eye to check the world for people in need. From 3:00-6:00 p.m., he met and talked with visitors and taught the dharma. The Buddha was a master teacher who excelled in "giving joy to the wise, promoting the intelligence of the average people and dispelling the darkness of the dull-witted."

The First Watch	(6.00 p.m. to 10.00 p.m.)

The Buddha continued to speak, teach, and lecture all who were interested.

The Middle Watch	(10.00 p.m. to 2.00 a.m.)

This period was reserved for devas to ask the Buddha questions. Although devas are in the highest realm and enjoy many sensory pleasures, they are not enlightened and so are frantically attempting to extinguish their remaining fetters, attain nirvana, and avoid being thrown into a lower realm.

The Last Watch	(2.00 a.m. to 4.00 a.m.)

From 2:00-3:00 a.m., the Buddha did walking meditation and stretched his muscles that were tight from sitting all day. Then, as he did during his entire forty-five-year ministry, he slept for one hour only.[433]

Yasodhara. Entered an arranged marriage with her cousin Siddhartha Gautama when both were sixteen. Described as a beautiful young woman, at the age of twenty-nine, she gave birth to a boy, Rahula. Seven days later, Siddhartha left to seek enlightenment. Yasodhara was later among the five hundred women, led by the Buddha's stepmother Prajapati, who were ordained in the original Order of Bhikkunis. She became an arahat. Yasodhara died, at the age of seventy-eight, two years before the Buddha's parinirvanization.

References

Armstrong, K. (2001). <u>Buddha.</u> New York: Penguin

Bercholz, S. and Kohn, S.C. (Eds.). (1993). <u>The Buddha and his teachings</u>. Boston, MA: Shambhala Publications, Inc.

Bodhi, B. (ed.). (2003). <u>Great disciples of the Buddha. Their lives, their works, their legacy</u>. Somerville, MA: Wisdom Publications.

Burt, E.A. (1955). <u>The teaching of the compassionate Buddha</u>. New York: Mentor Books.

Burton, N., Hart, Brother P, & Laughlin, J. (Eds.). (1975. <u>The Asian journal of Thomas Merton</u>. New York: New Directions Publishing Corporation.

Carus, P. (1998). <u>The teachings of Buddha</u>. (Rev. ed.) New York: St. Martin's Press.

Chang, G.C.C. (Translator). (1962). <u>The Hundred Thousand Songs of Milarepa</u>. (Volume 1.) Boston: Shambhala Publications Inc.

Chopra, D. (2007). <u>Buddha. A story of enlightenment</u>. New York: Harper One.

DeCaroli, R. (2015). Image problems: The origin and development of the Buddha's image in early south Asia. Seattle: University of Washington Press, eBook.

Dhamma, R. Dr. (1997). The first discourse of the Buddha. Boston: Wisdom Publications.

Easwaran, E. (Translator). (1985). The Dhammapada. Tomales, CA: Nilgiri Press.

EC Buddhism: Buddha: Untold Story - Who Killed Gautama?

Elliot, N. (Translator). (2002). Shantideva's Guide to the Bodhisattva's Way of Life. Ulverston, England: Tharpa Publications.

Erricker, C. (1995). Buddhism. London: Hodder Headline Plc.

Gethin, R. (1998). The foundations of Buddhism. New York: Oxford University Press.

Gethin, R. (2008). Sayings of the Buddha. New York: Oxford University Press.

Goddard, D. (Ed.). (1966). A Buddhist Bible. Boston: Beacon Press.

Hecker, H. (2003). Ananda. Guardian of the Dhamma. In N. Thera & H. Hecker (Eds.), Great disciples of the Buddha. Their lives, their works, their legacy (pp. 139-182). Somervillé,

MA: Wisdom Publications.https://dhammawiki.com/index.php?title=32_signs_of_a_great_man

Lee, Hon Sing. (Oct. 13, 2002.). Ten eminent disciples of the Buddha. http://honsing.com/Disciples.htm

Lopez Jr., D.S. (Ed.). (2004). <u>Buddhist scriptures</u>. London: Penguin Books Ltd.

Lyon, Q.M. (1957). <u>The great religions</u>. New York: The Odyssey Press, Inc.

Maguire, J. (2001). <u>Essential Buddhism. A complete guide to beliefs and practices</u>. New York: Pocket Books.

Marcus, Rabbi Yossi. (Sep. 23, 2005). Why are many things in Judaism done three times? http://www.askmoses.com/en/article/228,503/Why-are-many-things-in-Judaism-done-three-times.html

Moore, G.F. (1920). <u>History of religions</u>. New York: Charles Scribner's Sons.

Olendski, A. (2005). Translator. <u>Ananda Thera: Ananda Alone</u>. https://accesstoinsight.org/tipitaka/kn/thag/thag.17.03.olen.html

OSHO. (2004). <u>Buddha. His life and teachings and impact on humanity</u>. Switzerland: OSHO International Foundation.

Palikanon. <u>Ananda.</u> http://www.palikanon.com

Rahula, W. (1959). <u>What the Buddha taught</u>. (Rev. ed.) New York: Grove Press.

Ray, R.A. (2001). <u>Secret of the Vajra world.</u> Boston: Shambhala.

Revered Wisdom: <u>Buddhism.</u> (2010). New York: Sterling Publishing Co.

Saddhatissa, H. (1998). <u>Before he was Buddha: The life of Siddhartha</u>. Berkeley, CA: Seastone.

Sasaki, S.A. (1931). <u>The story of the giant disciples of Buddha: Ananda and Maha-Kasyapa</u>. Kessinger Legacy Reprints.

Shakespeare, W. (1994). <u>William Shakespeare. The complete works</u>. New York: MetroBooks.

Skilton, A. (1994). <u>A concise history of Buddhism</u>. New York: Barnes & Noble Books.

Smith, H. (1958). <u>The religions of man</u>. New York: Harper & Row.

Smith, H. (1991). <u>The world's religions</u>. New York: Harper Collins.

Smith, H. and Novak, P. (2003). <u>Buddhism. A Concise Introduction</u>. San Francisco: HarperCollins.

Snelling, J. (1987). <u>The Buddhist handbook. A complete guide to Buddhist teaching and practice.</u> London: Rider.

Stone, J.I. and Cuevas, B.J. 2007). <u>The Buddhist dead: Practices, discourses, representations.</u> From the Kuroda Institute series: Studies in east Asian Buddhism, vol. 20. Honolulu: University of Hawaii Press, ebook.

Strong, J.S. (2001). <u>The Buddha: A short biography</u>. Oxford: Oneworld Publications.

Strong, J.S. (2009). <u>The Buddha. A beginner's guide</u>. London: Oneworld Publications.

TBE <u>Tibetan Buddhist Encyclopedia</u>. <u>Ananda - Tibetan Buddhist Encyclopedia</u>

THAG. <u>https://tipitaka.fandom.com/wiki/Thag 17.3 PTS: Thag 1034-36 Ananda Thera: Ananda Alone(excerpt)</u>

Trungpa, C. (1987). <u>Cutting Through Spiritual Materialism</u>. Boston: Shambhala Publications Inc.

Wallis, G. (2007). <u>Basic teachings of the Buddha</u>. New York: The Modern Library.

Walser, J. (2005). <u>Mahayana Buddhism and early Indian culture</u>. New York: Columbia University Press.

Watson, B. (Trans.). (1988). <u>The Lotus Sutra</u>. New York: Columbia University Press.

Watson, B. (Trans.). (1997). <u>The Vimalakirti Sutra</u>. New York: Columbia University Press.

Yeshe, Y. and Zopa, Lama Rinpoche. (2000). <u>Wisdom energy. Basic Buddhist teachings</u>. Boston: Wisdom Publications.

About the Author

Randall K. Scott has been a practicing Buddhist for fifteen years. He taught at the university-level for forty years and retired in 2020 as Professor and Chair Emeritus. He has numerous scholarly publications, as well as a novel, <u>Ring a Ring of Roses</u>. Supported by extensive references, Dr. Scott brings a fresh, unique approach to this examination of Ananda's life. The book also includes a brief introduction to Buddhism, the Four Noble Truths, the Noble Eightfold Path, The Buddha's Ten Most Influential Disciples, and a glossary of Buddhist terminology. Dr. Scott, his wife Marc'a, and their miniature schnauzer Archie, live in Alabama. He can be reached at ellenkieth1@gmail.com.

Endnotes

Introduction

1 Lopez, 2004, 191
2 Lopez, 2004,123
3 Burton et al, 244

Chapter 1

4 TBE 3
5 www.burmese-art.com/blog/
  ten-great-disciples
6 TBE 1
7 Hecker 139
8 Lee, 2002, 3
9 Strong, 2001, 123
10 Goddard 122.
11 Snelling, 3
12 Lee 3
13 Lee 5
14 Sasaki, 14
15 THAG 2

Chapter 2

16 OSHO 50
17 OSHO 52
18 OSHO 52
19 Armstrong 133
20 Lee 1
21 Smith, 1958, 88
22 Bodhi 163
23 Lopez 124
24 Lopez 279
25 Skilton 63
26 Smith and Novak 75
27 Lee 6

Chapter 3

28 TBE 3
29 Palikanon 1
30 Palikanon 1
31 Bodhi 139
32 Sasaki 7
33 OSHO 49
34 Sasaki 8
35 Sasaki 7
36 Palikanon 1-2
37 OSHO 53
38 Sasaki 7
39 Sasaki 9
40 Sasaki 9
41 Sasaki 9
42 Bodhi 152
43 THAG 2
44 THAG 2
45 Bodhi 163
46 THAG 2
47 Bodhi 148
48 Sadd. 78
49 Bodhi 148
50 Palkanon 2, BBE 3
51 Snelling 37
52 Sadd 94-95
53 THAG 2
54 Snelling 39
55 Palikanon 2
56 Palikanon 5
57 Bodhi 142.
58 Bodhi 140

59   TBE 1
60   Bodhi 140
61   Bodhi 160
62   Bodhi 160-161
63   Revered 91
64   Sadd 102-103
65   Burton et al 364
66   Bodhi 150
67   Bodhi 151
68   Bodhi 151
69   TBE 1
70   Bodhi 161
71   Bodhi 161
72   Bodhi 162
73   Bodhi 162
74   Bodhi 141
75   Bodhi 142
76   Palikanon 3
77   Bodhi 143
78   Bodhi 140
79   Bodhi 161
80   Strong, 2001, 118
81   Bodhi 157
82   Bodhi 162
83   Bodhi 145
84   Watson 154
85   Watson 154-155
86   Watson 155
87   Watson 155
88   Watson 156
89   Watson 157
90   Watson 157
91   Watson 158
92   Watson158
93   Watson 159
94   Bodhi, 2003, 145
95   Bodhi, 2003, 145-146
96   Sadd 119
97   Sadd 120
98   Bodhi, 2003, 149
99   Palikanon 4
100 Palikanon 4

Chapter 4
101 Lyon 176
102 Bercholz 7

103 Bercholz 7
104 Bercholz 8
105 Bercholz 9
106 Bercholz 9-10
107 Bercholz 10
108 Strong, 2001, 55
109 Bercholz 10
110 Bercholz 10
111 Moore 298
112 Moore 298
113 Easwaran 37
114 Snelling, 33
115 Strong 2001 122
116 Strong 2001 122
117 Bodhi 154
118 Easwaran 36
119 Snelling, 33-34
120 Easwaran 37
121 Moore 289
122 Easwaran 37
123 Easwaran 37-38
124 Easwaran 38
125 Easwaran 38
126 Easwaran 38
127 Bodhi 155
128 Sadd 79
129 *https://www.budsas.org/ebud/*
     rdbud/rdbud-01.htm
130 Snelling 34; Bodhi 155
131 Armstrong 159
132 Lee 5
133 TBE 3

Chapter 5
134 Sasaki 14
135 Lee 5
136 Bodhi 156
137 Bodhi 156
138 Bodhi 156
139 Bodhi 156
140 Sasaki 14
141 Goddard 110
142 Goddard 110
143 Sasaki 14
144 Sasaki 14
145 Sasaki 14

146 Sasaki 14
147 Goddard 110
148 Goddard 110
149 Sasaki 14
150 Sasaki 14
151 Sasaki 14
152 Sasaki 15
153 Goddard 109-110
154 Goddard 110
155 Goddard 110
156 Sasaki 15
157 Sasaki 15
158 Goddard 111
159 Sasaki 16
160 Sasaki 16
161 Sasaki 16
162 Sasaki 16
163 Sasaki 16
164 Sasaki 16
165 Sasaki 16
166 Sasaki 16-17
167 Sasaki 17
168 Sasaki 17
169 Sasaki 17
170 Goddard 111
171 Goddard 111
172 Goddard 111-112
173 Goddard 112
174 Goddard 112
175 Goddard 114
176 Goddard 122
177 Goddard 122
178 Goddard 122
179 Goddard 122-123
180 Goddard 125
181 Goddard 125
182 Goddard 127
183 Goddard 127
184 Goddard 127
185 Goddard 129
186 Goddard 129
187 Goddard 129
188 Goddard 149
189 Goddard 149-150
190 Goddard 197-198

191 Goddard 199
192 Goddard 263
193 Goddard 263
194 Goddard 264
195 Goddard 270
196 Goddard 271
197 Goddard 271
198 Goddard 275
199 Bodhi 137
200 Bodhi 144
201 Bodhi 144
202 Bodhi 144
203 Bodhi 159
204 Bodhi 159
205 Bodhi 159-160
206 Bodhi 160
207 Bodhi 160
208 Bodhi 160

Chapter 6
209 Strong, 2001, 130
210 Goddard 14
211 Strong, 2001, 130
212 Strong, 2001, 130
213 Strong, 2001, 130-131
214 Goddard 14
215 Strong, 2001, 130-131
216 Strong, 2001, 135
217 " Moore, 290
218 Bercholz, 1993, 41
219 Bercholz, 1993, 41
220 Bercholz 1993 41
221 Bercholz, 1993, 42
222 Bodhi 171
223 Bodhi 171
224 Strong, 2001, 133
225 Bodhi 171
226 Bodhi 169
227 Bodhi 169
228 Lee 2002

Chapter 7
229 Revered 87
230 Gethin, 2008, 72
231 Snelling 39
232 Gethin, 2008, 72
233 Armstrong 179

234 Sadd 123
235 Gethin, 2008, 72
236 Revered 87
237 Gethin, 2008, 72
238 Maguire 20
239 Maguire 138
240 Bercholz 42
241 Armstrong 179
242 Goddard 15
243 EC Buddhism: Search results for
     lick-spittle
244 Strong, 2001, 95
245 Armstrong 176
246 Sasaki 9
247 Strong, 2001, 135-136
248 Gethin, 2008, 73
249 Armstrong 180
250 Gethin, 2008, 73
251 Gethin, 2008, 73
252 Gethin, 2008, 74
253 Carus 124
254 Gethin, 2008, 76-77
255 Caras 124
256 Caras 124
257 Caras 124
258 Gethin, 2008, 77
259 Gethin, 2008, 78
260 Snelling 39
261 Gethin, 2008, 78
262 Maguire 21
263 Strong, 2001, 137
264 Revered 88
265 Strong, 2001 137
266 Easwaran 44-45
267 Gethin 80
268 Gethin 81
269 Strong 2001 180
270 Caras 126
271 Gethin, 2008, 82
272 Caras 124
273 Sasaki, 12
274 Gethin, 2008, 83
275 Gethin, 2008, 83
276 Gethin, 2008, 84
277 Gethin, 2008, 84

278 Gethin, 2008, 85
279 Gethin, 2008, 85
280 Gethin, 2008, 86
281 Gethin, 2008, 88
282 Gethin, 2008, 81
283 Gethin, 2008, 81
284 Gethin, 2008, 81
285 Strong, 1995, 36
286 Caras 127
287 Carus 127
288 Bodhi 176
289 Bodhi 176
290 Revered 91
291 Gethin, 2008, 88-89
292 Gethin, 2008, 89
293 Gethin, 2008, 89
294 Gethin, 2008, 89
295 Burt 49
296 Bodhi 177
297 Revered 90

298 Bodhi 177
299 Maguire 20
300
301 Gethin, 2008, 90
302 Strong, 2001, 184
303 Bodhi 177
304 Gethin, 2008, 90
305 Gethin, 2008, 91
306 Bodhi 178
307 DeCaroli 1
308 DeCaroli 1
309 Strong 2001 143
310 Strong, 2001, 143
311 Revered 92
312 Revered 93
313 Strong, 2001, 143
314 Strong, 2001, 144
315 Strong, 2001, 144
316 Revered 93
317 Lopez 124
318 Strong 2001 144
319 Revered 93
320 Revered 93
321 Lopez 124

322 Revered 94

Chapter 8

323 Lopez 124
324 ." Lopez 124
325 Sadd 124
326 Lopez 124
327 Lopez 125
328 Lopez 125
329 Smith & Novak 74
330 Lopez 126
331 THAG
332 Sasaki 11
333 TBE 5
334 Bodhi 140-141
335 Sasaki 10
336 Bodhi 144
337 Bodhi 144
338 Bodhi 144
339 Bodhi 179-180
340 THAG 2
341 Bodhi 148
342 Snelling 81
343 Skilton, 45
344 Bodhi 131
345 Bodhi 179
346 Bodhi 179
347 Sadd 124, TBE 4
348 Sadd 125
349 Maguire, 2001, 37
350 Hecker, 2003, 180
351 TBE 4
352 Lee 2002
353 Hecker, 2003, 180
354 Bodhi 180
355 Strong, 2001, 107
356 Bodhi 180

Chapter 9

357 Sasaki, 7
358 TBE 5
359 Smith & Novak 74
360 TBE 4
361 Sasaki, 7
362 Strong, 2001, 192
363 Sasaki 7
364 Sadd 124

365 Sadd 125
366 Sadd 125
367 Bodhi 180
368 Skilton 46
369 TBE 4
370 Bodhi 180-181
371 TBE 4
372 Strong, 2001, 143
373 Sadd 78

Chapter 10

374 Bodhi 182
375 TBE 4
376 THAG 17.3
377 Sasaski, 17
378 Sasaki 17
379 Bodhi 141
380 Sasaki, 17-18
381 Bodhi 182, Lee 6, THAG 2
382 Lee 7
383 Sasaki 18
384 Sasaki 18
385 TBE 4
386 Lee 7
387 Sasaki 18

Chapter 11

388 TBE 1
389 TBE 4
390 Thag 1041-1044
391 Bodhi 153
392 Sasaki 9
393 Sasaki 9-10
394 Shakespeare, 508
395 Lopez 416

Chapter 12

396 Erricker, 24
397 Strong 2001 63
398 Snelling 25
399 Strong 2001, 67-68
400 Strong 2001 69
401 Erricker 24
402 Revered 102
403 Erricker 25
404 Revered 103
405 Strong, 2001, 73
406 Erricker 27

407 .*https://www.freepressjournal.
in/webspecial/guru-purnima-
2019-mythological-significance-
buddhist-history-tithi-and-all-you-
need-to-know*

Chapter 13

408 OSHO 43

409 TBE 4

410 https://buddhistpage.com/venerable-
anandacustodian-of-the-dhamma.

Glossary

411 Anuttara-samyak-sambodhi - Tibetan
Buddhist Encyclopedia

412 Armstrong 181

413 https://www.livescience.com/60933-
cremated-remains-of-buddha-found.
html

414 Marcus, 2005

415 Strong, 2001, 40

416 Gethin, 1998, 31-32.

417 Strong, 2001, 57

418 Life of Buddha: The Mirror of the
Dhamma (Part 2) (buddhanet.net)

419 Sadd 13

420 Sadd 71

421 https://www.budsas.org/ebud/rdbud/
rdbud-01.htm

422 Smith & Novak, 60

423 Smith & Novak 52-53

424 Strong, 2001, 125

425 http://www.
chinabuddhismencyclopedia.com/en/
index.php/King_Pasenadi_Kosala

426 Gethin 171-172

427 Gethin, 1998, 119-119.

428 Yeshe and Zopa 82-85

429 Easwaran 132

430 Goddard 15

431 Gethin, 1998, 73

432 Flower Said to Bloom Once in
3,000 Years Spotted Across Globe
(theepochtimes.com)

433 **http://www.buddhanet.
net/e-learning/buddhism/
lifebuddha/26lbud.htm**

Index

as from warrior caste, 25
behaviors/activities of
   becoming wandering
      mendicant, xiv
   choosing Ananda as his personal
      attendant, 13
   as choosing to walk rather than
      ride, xv
   experimentation with
      fasting, xiv
   mysterious distant journeys
      of, 27
   as not considering social caste
      when admitting men to
      sangha, 8
   number-one priority of, xvi
   as often saying something
      enigmatic or ambiguous, 20
   as predicting Ananda's destiny,
      30, 31
   as promoting all things in
      moderation, 9
   as rescuing hundred-thousand
      beings, xv
   as revealing that another
      Buddha will appear, 87
   as spending much of his
      time putting out fires and
      settling disagreements among
      followers, 10
   as struggling with same
      problems we deal with
      today, 23
   as summing up Ananda's
      difficulties in reaching
      enlightenment, 58
   use of Socratic Method by, 43
   as wanting a personal attendant,
      12–13
   years of preaching the
      dharma, 12
defined, 143

discourses of
   accuracy of, 144
   public demand for discourses
      of, 11
later years of
   as attaining final nibbana, 91
   on deciding when he was going
      into full extinction, 68–69
   declining health of, 65–71
   final days of, 88
   final words of, 89–90
   harbinger of death of, 16
   last meal of, 73–74, 79
   parinirvanization of, xv, xvi, 71,
      72–94, 151
   as physically worn out, 12
as one of Three Jewels, 174
post-parinirvanization of
   cremation of, 94
   mourning of, 92–93
   pre-cremation scene of, 93
   veneration of, 94
requirements of disciples, 7–8
traits/characteristics of
   as able to see the future, 77
   as earning his enlightenment by
      self-discovery, 103
   enlightenment of, xiv, xv,
      xvi, 151
   as having enormous patience
      with Ananda, 119
   as not a god, xiii, 9, 25
   as not the hard-core misogynist
      he is characterized as by some
      historians, 67
   place of enlightenment, 81, 151
   thirty-two signs of as marking
      him as having attained
      complete Buddhahood, 2
   as transcending this world, xiv
   as very strong-willed, 43
and women

assassination attempts on Buddha
by, 76

Buddha's cousin, 26

as Buddha's nemesis, 74

as prime suspect in assassination
of Buddha (if Buddha was
assassinated), 75

psychosis of, 26

devas/celestial beings (gods), 167

Dhamma, 21, 22, 27, 42, 45, 48, 49,
62, 67, 87, 90, 91, 96–97, 100, 103,
147, 151, 173

Dhammapada, 171

Dharma

Buddha-dharma, 143

defined, 11, 149

as fully revealed, 68

as holding answers to
enlightenment, 72

Mirror of Dharma, 65, 158–159

as one of Three Jewels, 8, 11, 174

restoration of, 143

teaching of, 12, 19, 41, 115, 126,
129, 130, 142, 177

dhyana/jhana, 60, 90, 149, 173

disciples

most as not literate, 10

power struggles, turf wars, and
personality clashes among, 8–9

requirements of, 7–8

as struggling with same problems
we deal with today, 23

ten most influential ones, 129–132

duality, 83, 149–150

dukkha, 38, 134, 137, 150. *See also* First
Noble Truth (Dukkha)

E

emptiness (sunyata), 150

enlightenment

of Ananda, 104, 105–106

of arhats, 13, 103

as attained by one's own efforts,
29, 76

as available to all, 68

of Buddha, xiv, xv, xvi, 103, 151

defined, 150

Dharma as holding answers to, 72

of disciples, 12–13

downside of attaining, 118

as not eliminating all desires and
emotions, 24

as not requiring total abandonment
of loving kindness, 118

of Rahula, 117

side effect of as losing one's sense of
humor, 101

existence, realms of, 166–171

F

fasting, Buddha's recognition of it
as not only ineffective in reaching
nirvana but also very dangerous, 107

First Noble Truth (Dukkha), 38, 126,
134, 150, 171. *See also* dukkha

five precepts, 150–151

Flaming Mouth (hungry ghost), 121

food poisoning, as rampant and often
fatal, 74

Four Noble Truths

acceptance of, 8

Buddha as providing road map
through, 80, 83, 126, 127

described, 133–136

difficulty in understanding and
penetrating, 25

study of, 153–154

teaching of, xv

four places every Buddhist should visit,
81, 151

Fourth Noble Truth, 135–136, 137

the Four Sights, 21, 39, 151

friendship, importance of, according to
Buddha, 24

T

Tathagata, 42, 59, 61, 68, 69, 72, 73, 79, 81, 82, 83, 84, 85, 86, 89, 120, 165, 173

Tejokasina, 115, 173

ten fetters/bonds, 163, 173–174

Tenzin Gyatso (Dalai Lama), 148

Theravada (sect of Buddhism), 139, 142, 143, 147, 152, 155, 163, 174

Third Noble Truth, 135

Three Jewels, 172, 174

thus have I heard/thus I have heard, 108, 175

Tipitaka/Tripitaka (three baskets), 108, 163, 175. *See also* Abhidamma/ Abhidharma; Sutra; Vinaya

Tree of Awakening (Bodhi Tree), 19, 142–143

trial of Ananda, 109–111

Tusita heaven, 2, 93, 156, 167, 175

U

Udayi/Udayin (disciple), 28, 29, 147

Udumbara tree, 175

Upali, 105, 131, 147

Upatissa (disciple), 10, 159. *See also* Sariputra/Upatissa

Upavana (monk), 81, 82

upsaka (masculine) upasika (feminine), 176

V

Vangisa (poet), 62–64

Vedic period/Vedic age, 176

Vesali/Vaisali, 36, 65, 66, 72, 115

viceroy, 5, 176

Vinaya, as one of three baskets for organizing Buddhist theology, 11, 48, 87, 96–97, 108, 111, 131, 143, 147, 175, 176

Visuddhimagga (Path of Purification) (Buddhaghosa), 144

W

watches, 79, 82, 84, 176–177

wisdom, as steps 1 and 2 of Noble Eightfold Path, 137

women
  Ananda's attraction to, 49
  Buddha as maintaining wariness of, 87
  Buddha as opposed to women in the sangha, xv–xvi, 8
  Buddha as pressured to admit women into sangha, 8, 17, 19, 41, 46
  in Buddha's life, 38–41
  as finding Ananda attractive, 48
  as having no rights, xv
  life of homelessness and seeking enlightenment a not considered viable option for, 46
  as powerless in Siddhartha's society, 40
  in the sangha, 37–47
  social movement to admit women into sangha intensifying, 41

Y

Yasodhara, Siddhartha's wife, 25, 38, 40, 42, 43–44, 107, 147, 177